THE CHURCH IN THE THOUGHT
OF BISHOP JOHN ROBINSON

The Church
in the Thought
of Bishop John Robinson

RICHARD P. McBRIEN

THE WESTMINSTER PRESS
Philadelphia

First Published 1966

LIBRARY OF CONGRESS CATALOG CARD NO. 66–23087

Published by The Westminster Press®
Philadelphia, Pennsylvania

PRINTED IN THE UNITED STATES OF AMERICA

CONTENTS

I · THE NATURE OF THE CHURCH

II · THE MISSION OF THE CHURCH

FOREWORD

by Bishop John A. T. Robinson

IT is with real pleasure that I write this foreword in appreciation of Fr McBrien's book. He has written of my work with very great understanding and sympathy, and I can testify to the endless trouble he has taken to be accurate and fair. I suppose it is still a surprise in these early years of ecumenical thaw to find such a degree of interest and concern across the barrier that has hitherto insulated Roman Catholic from non-Roman theology and mission. I welcome too the perspective which so informed and intelligent an outsider to the Anglican tradition has been able to bring. As far as I know, no one else has seriously attempted to see how *Honest to God* fits into the context of my other theological writings. Indeed, I have had so little time to reflect on the process myself that I have found the emerging pattern illuminating.

One remark in particular has caught my attention. Fr McBrien observes what he calls 'a certain attrition' in my 'doctrine of the Church over the past ten years or so'. I can understand what he means. For I think I have less interest in the Church in and for itself. There has been a movement in my thought from essentialist to functional categories, from pure to applied theology. This is partly, I suspect, a movement characteristic of our whole age, partly a shift in the *place* in which my theology has been done. For I would agree with Harvey Cox when he writes in a recent article:[1] '*What* we think is determined far more than we realize by *where* we think (our "Sitz im Denken") and *why* we think (the *aim* of our theological enquiry).' And he goes on to say: 'The purpose of theology is to serve the prophetic community. For this reason the place of theology is that jagged edge where the faithful company grapples with the swiftest currents of the age. Any "theology" which occurs somewhere else or for some other reason scarcely deserves the name.'

That may be an exaggeration; but I believe it describes the norm. And by that norm I doubt whether the word 'attrition' is the right

[1] 'The Place and Purpose of Theology,' *The Christian Century*, January 5, 1966, p. 7.

one. The process is legitimately seen as a wearing or whittling away only
when regarded from the point of view of a different norm, which has
in fact dominated the perspective of theology in all our ecclesiastical
traditions. In this perspective the 'jagged edge', so far from being
the proper place of theological engagement, represents the point
furthest out, the position *in extremis* for which the norm must be
flexible enough to allow. In such a situation, it is recognized, much may
indeed have to go by the board; but spend too much time in it and
serious attrition is bound to result.

One of the valuable features of Fr McBrien's treatment is the way
in which he has detected the continuing influence on my thinking
of the formula, going back a long way, which may be expressed by
saying: 'Have as high a doctrine of the Ministry as you like, as long
as your doctrine of the Church is higher; and have as high a doctrine
of the Church as you like, as long as your doctrine of the Kingdom
is higher.' This subordination of the Ministry to the Church and
of the Church to the Kingdom has affected the perspective of all
my writings. It has meant that I have never been interested in the
Church or in a doctrine of the Church for its own sake. Even my
'purest' academic study of the subject, *The Body*, had an Introduction
which took its start from George Orwell's *Nineteen-eighty-four*. And
this movement has been accentuated since.

It is, however, a movement that runs counter to the approach
which has shaped the priorities of most theological writing and
thinking on the doctrine of the Church. This has been governed by
the simple fact that the vast majority of those who have engaged
in it have not only been churchmen, with a primary interest in life
inside rather than outside the Church, but clergy. Starting from
where they are, their way in almost inevitably has been through a
concern with the Ministry – witness the dominant preoccupation
in ecumenical talks, at any rate until quite recently, with questions
of the Ministry that have left the laity largely unmoved. From there
the discussion has broadened out to a rediscovery of the *laos* or whole
People of God and their part in the Church's liturgy and mission.
And from the *laos* and the liturgy there has been a way through to a
new understanding of society and the secular. But still in most theological writing, church papers or ecclesiastical debate one would never

begin to guess that the laity constituted 99.5 per cent of the Church. They appear much more like a penumbra, occupying the area between the clerical nucleus and the so-called 'outside' world.

This approach has been true of all our traditions, but of none more explicitly – and indeed unashamedly – than of the dominant ethos of the Roman Catholic Church. The laity have been regarded as complementary to the hierarchy and almost need not have existed for the essential structure of the Church to survive. For many practical purposes the Church has been identified with the Ministry, and the Kingdom of God with the Church – the latter being diagnosed by Anglicans like F. D. Maurice and T. O. Wedel as the fundamental error of the Church of Rome.

The transition from Vatican I to Vatican II registers the swing of the Roman Catholic Church away from both these identifications. And it is a process that is obviously not finished. Indeed, the significance of the Decrees of Vatican II lies in the movement (and the momentum) they reflect, not in the particular point which this happened to have reached when the vote was taken and the ink dried. The great hope lies in the fact that they determined nothing, but left the ends open.

Yet when all has been said, they still reflect the traditional theological order of God–Church–World (and indeed of God–Ministry-Church–World), as if God were primarily at work in his Church and through that on the world. Whereas, the biblical order (as the more radical material from the World Council of Churches' Commission on the Missionary Structure of the Congregation insists) is, rather, God-World–Church. The primary obedience of the Church is to find out where 'the action' is, to be sensitive to the points at which God is working in history on the frontiers of social change, and there to serve him in it. And this approach is increasingly represented not only in the Protestant sphere (Harvey Cox's book *The Secular City* is a notable example of it), but within the Roman Catholic Communion by men like Rahner, Congar, de Chardin, and indeed by Fr McBrien himself.

According to which end of the telescope one looks through, issues will tend to loom large or appear relatively insignificant. The eye-piece of Vatican II, however improved the range of its vision, is still at the ecclesiastical end, and its central decree on the Church continues to reflect this perspective. As Dom Aelred Graham put it in an article for a secular journal,[2] 'Who but the clergy, or ecclesiastically minded laymen, could conceivably be interested in a topic that is apparently of absorbing concern to the Council participants – the "collegiality" of bishops?'

This is not to carp, but to draw out the fact that however far we have gone – any of us – we have hardly begun. The doctrine of the Church has never consistently been worked out from the end of the Kingdom: the Kingdom has regularly been seen from the end of the Church. There are signs of real movements in the other direction – and characteristically and hopefully they cut right across our established ecclesiastical lines. From these lines, indeed, they are bound to appear reductionist. But I see them, as the stirrings of a rather, genuinely 'lay 'theology (taking its start from the involvement of 'the prophetic community' in the world), which I believe to be the distinctive call to the Church of this generation.

It is the kind of theology for which a bishop is of all men in many ways the least well 'placed'. His very liturgy and ministry at the centre of the ecclesiastical circle compel him to see close up the things which in perspective should be subordinate – not, in their place, less important, but subordinate. Indeed, in our present situation, where the idea of a missionary bishop on the frontier of the secular world is a strange category, one often feels as if one is looking down opposite ends of a telescope with each eye. This is a distracting exercise. But it may be a necessary part of the burden of transition. For a true understanding of the nature and mission of the Church is, I believe, possible in our day only if it is accepted that one has to start looking at almost every aspect of it – liturgy, ministry, spirituality, structure, and the rest – also 'from the other end'. What this will involve in the *next* 'ten years or so' is likely to mean more than a little 'attrition'. It may require of us all, whatever our ecclesiastical allegiance, a much more radical shift of perspective than has marked the revolution even of this last decade.

[2] 'The Pathos of Vatican II,' *Encounter*, December 1965, p. 17.

PREFACE

THE purpose of this book is to examine the ecclesiology of John A. T. Robinson, Anglican bishop of Woolwich, in the light of some current developments in Catholic, Anglican and Protestant theology. No attempt is made to disguise the fact that Bishop Robinson is neither a professional theologian nor a systematic ecclesiologist. How, then, is this investigation to be justified and what might be its relevance?

To say that Robinson is not a *professional* theologian is true, but misleading. Bishop Robinson is, and has always been, engaged in the theological enterprise in a profoundly serious manner. He lectured for three years on doctrinal theology, New Testament, and social ethics at an Anglican theological college, and lectured for an even longer period in the field of New Testament studies at Cambridge. His writings, in the Cambridge years especially, were devoted to exegesis and biblical theology, and were of a serious scientific nature. But simultaneously Robinson was publishing works of a less academic character, pastoral in tone and markedly ecclesiological in content. *On Being the Church in the World*[1] and *Liturgy Coming to Life*[2] are such products of this Cambridge period. After his consecration as bishop of Woolwich in 1959, his abiding interest in matters of pastoral import intensified under the impact of his new episcopal responsibilities. 'How shall the Gospel be relevant in mid-twentieth century secular society?' 'What is to be the place and mission of the Church in this new situation?' These questions, always of concern to him, have assumed a new urgency, and he has attempted to provide some tentative answers in his most recent books, *Honest to God*[3] and *The New Reformation?*[4] Neither of

[1] London: SCM Press, 1960.

[2] London: Mowbray, 1960 (2nd ed., 1963). Except for references to the *preface* of the second edition, page references in this study are from the 1960 edition.

[3] London: SCM Press, 1963.

[4] London: SCM Press, 1965.

these volumes are works of professional theology in the sense of the *Church Dogmatics* of Karl Barth or the *Systematic Theology* of Paul Tillich, to cite but two examples in the Protestant tradition. But to admit that Robinson's recent writings are less systematic is not to suggest necessarily that they are less serious or less profound. They represent, it seems to me, what Charles Davis has referred to as 'episcopal theology', that is to say, a theology 'strongly marked by the pastoral concern of the Church'.[5] 'There is a contribution to theology', Father Davis continues, 'that can be made only by bishop-theologians. The fact that no bishop, however theologically minded, would bother with some of the questions discussed by theologians would have a purifying effect on theology were bishops more closely involved in theological activity than they are.'[6]

The theologian's task, Davis writes elsewhere, is 'historically conditioned and he must begin from its present embodiment. Any creative theology arises out of the actual life of the Church. The real theological questions are always contemporary and, moreover, they can be effectively handled only by someone who is sensitive to the present action of the Spirit in the Church.'[7]

Neither is Bishop Robinson a *systematic* ecclesiologist – and this is even more obvious. He has never attempted to produce a coherent, detailed, logically ordered doctrine of the Church. Yet it is my contention that ecclesiological concerns are paramount throughout his published works, and that his writings in this area are sufficiently consistent and explicit to allow one to develop a synthesis by induction.

There are at least three reasons to support the relevance of this study. First, Anglicanism has always occupied a central place in the ecumenical movement and any indications of new directions or shifts of emphasis within the Anglican Church would have immediate ecumenical import. Secondly, Bishop Robinson's understanding of the Church has been influenced strongly by the biblical, liturgical, and ecumenical movements. Catholic ecclesiology has been, and

---

[5] 'Theology in Seminary Confinement', *Downside Review* 81 (1963) 310.
[6] *Idem.*
[7] 'Theology and its Present Task', in *Theology and the University: an ecumenical investigation* (ed. J. Coulson), London: Darton, Longman and Todd, 1964, p. 109.

will continue to be, subject to these same currents of renewal. His work, then, might very well be indicative, or even prognostic, of further developments within Catholic ecclesiology. Finally – and most significantly – Robinson stands as a symbol of the current ferment, or crisis (it has been described in various ways), within the body of mid-twentieth-century Christianity. The phenomenon of 'secular Christianity', so-called, and related questions, is something to be reckoned with. It is important that a theology – and, indeed, a Church – in crisis should have a firm and unshakable foundation. For a true radical, as Robinson himself would admit, is a man with roots. Reform and renewal without an adequate ecclesiological perspective is destined for failure. But one begs the question if one merely assumes that such is the case, that the present-day ferment in Anglican and Protestant theological circles is built on ecclesiological sand. It is precisely this question that we have chosen to confront in this book. John A. T. Robinson is a central figure in the effort to re-examine the presuppositions and assumptions of Christian theology. Without an adequate ecclesiology his own laudable hopes, and those of his colleagues, cannot achieve ultimate fulfilment.

This investigation will begin with a brief survey of the contemporary theological situation along with a consideration of the life and writings of Bishop Robinson in the context of this situation. This will be followed by an analysis and discussion of Robinson's understanding of the *nature* of the Church: his idea of the Church as the Body of Christ; his notion of the Church as the eschatological community; and, finally, the nature and function of the Church's ministry and liturgy. The consideration of these latter areas – ministry and liturgy – will provide a transition from the first part of the investigation to the second, for the ministry and, especially, the liturgy both reflect the nature of the Church as the Body of Christ and as the eschatological community, and also point to her mission in the world. Thus, in the second part of the study, there is a two-fold discussion of this *mission*: a discussion, on the one hand, of the function of the Church which arises specifically from the fact that she is a community in the world and in this age (that she is, in other words, a *secular* community); and an examination, on the other hand, of her mission to preach the Gospel (as the *missionary* community).[8] In every instance there will be an attempt to view the position of Bishop Robinson in the light of the current situation, in Catholic, Anglican, and Protestant theology. Particular reliance is placed on the recent declarations of the Second Vatican Council regarding the Church, the Liturgy, and Ecumenism.

In its original form this book was presented as a doctoral dissertation in Dogmatic Theology at the Gregorian University in Rome. For obvious practical reasons much of the original material and some of the scholarly apparatus had to be curtailed or eliminated outright in this published version. If this editing process has enhanced its readability, I hope that it has not diminished its usefulness as a serious critique of Bishop Robinson's doctrine of the Church. I regard Part Two of the book as the heart of this investigation, for it is in this area – namely, in treating of the question of the mission of the Church – that Bishop Robinson is making his most distinctive contribution to the contemporary debate in ecclesiology. Part One is designed to substantiate our position that the radical questions raised in *Honest to God* and *The New Reformation?* emanate from a theological starting-point that is 'conservative' in the best sense of that word.

There remains only the agreeable task of acknowledging assistance. I wish to express my appreciation, first of all, to the Reverend Angel Antón, S.J., professor of Ecclesiology at the Gregorian University in Rome, who served as the director of the doctoral dissertation from which this book has been produced. I also wish to thank the Reverend Francis A. Sullivan, S.J., dean of the Faculty of Theology at the Gregorian University, who served as 'second reader' for the thesis. I am indebted to them for their constructive criticisms.

A word of gratitude is due also to the library staffs of the Pontifical Biblical Institute in Rome, the Hartford Theological Seminary in

---

[8] Robinson himself describes the Christian community as *eschatological, missionary*, and *secular* in his published address, *The World that God Loves*, London: Church Missionary Society, 1963, p. 4. Nevertheless, the divisions that have been adopted are, to a certain extent at least, artificial. The schema serves a useful purpose, however, in making possible a more orderly and systematic study of Robinson's doctrine of the Church.

Connecticut, and finally to Dr Ans J. van der Bent, librarian of the World Council of Churches, Geneva.

An expression of appreciation is also gladly extended to the Most Reverend Henry J. O'Brien, Archbishop of Hartford, Connecticut, for graciously permitting me to join the faculty of the Pope John XXIII National Seminary in Weston, Massachusetts, and to His Eminence, Richard Cardinal Cushing, Archbishop of Boston, for generously sponsoring these years of graduate studies, of which this book is a result.

Finally, a special word of thanks is due to Bishop John A. T. Robinson himself for a truly admirable spirit of co-operation. Through correspondence and especially through a personal interview at his residence in London, he has aided immeasurably in the completion of this study. I am indebted to him for his helpful criticisms and suggestions and also for making available various articles and books which would otherwise have been very difficult to obtain, and particularly for providing me with the proofs – well in advance of publication – of his most recent book, *The New Reformation?* Nevertheless, despite his help and the assistance of those others whom I have mentioned above, I remain solely responsible for the final product in its entirety.

Pope John XXIII National Seminary   RICHARD P. MCBRIEN
Weston, Massachusetts

I

BISHOP ROBINSON AND THE
CONTEMPORARY THEOLOGICAL SITUATION

IT goes without saying – and, in fact, borders on the trite – to suggest that one cannot adequately assess the writings of a particular theologian (or, for that matter, any thinker at all) without taking into serious account the various factors – historical, theological, and even biographical – that have served to mould and shape his thought. The principle applies in a special manner to the published writings of Bishop John A. T. Robinson. Not himself the creative source of new currents of thought as, for example, were Karl Barth[1] and Rudolf Bultmann,[2] Robinson's originality consists in his ability to harness apparently divergent theological, philosophical, and sociological currents, and, through synthesis and modification, to employ these ideas for a new and sometimes altogether different purpose. This is particularly true of his much-publicized *Honest to God*,[3] for example. The reviewer of that book cannot afford to ignore its antecedents nor the theological context in which it was written, and those who have ignored these factors and have opted instead for a kind of fundamentalist rather than

[1] Cf. his *The Epistle to the Romans* (tr. E. Hoskyns from 6th ed.), Oxford: University Press, 1933. (1st ed., 1919.)

[2] Cf. his 'New Testament and Mythology', in *Kerygma and Myth* (ed. H. W. Bartsch; tr. R. H. Fuller), New York: Harper & Row, 1961. The essay originally appeared in 1941.

[3] London: SCM Press, 1963, p. 21: 'Indeed, it is the number of straws apparently blowing in the same direction that strikes me as significant. I have done little more than pick a few of them up and I am conscious that in this book, more than in any other I have written, I am struggling to think other people's thoughts after them.'

'form-critical' approach to the text have been too quick, it seems, to read the bishop out of the Christian community entirely.[4] *Honest to God* and its recent successor, *The New Reformation?*,[5] have not emanated from a theological vacuum. They are a part and, to an extent, a product of the contemporary theological situation. It is, therefore, imperative that the theological thought, and in particular the ecclesiology, of Bishop Robinson be discussed and evaluated in the light of this situation.

HISTORICAL CONTEXT[6]

The current ferment in the Church of England and in English theology generally – of which Bishop Robinson is so much a part – has its historical antecedents in the not-so-distant past. England was not always so closely attuned to or affected by philosophical and theological developments on the Continent. If anything, the French Revolution had served to stiffen her conservatism and deepen her insularity with respect to the new movements that were centred in Germany. By 1830, however, there was a different situation entirely. The Test Act had been repealed and Catholic Emancipation was a reality. The old ideal that Church and State in England were one society was a manifest anachronism. 'The Church needed a new infusion of spiritual life if it was to recover anything like its traditional standing and influence among the English people.'[7] It was into this vacuum that the Oxford Movement stepped, dominating the scene at least until 1845. By 1860 England was in turmoil again in the face of new developments in the biblical and the natural

---

[4] Cf., for example, O. F. Clarke, *For Christ's Sake*, Wallington: Religious Education Press, 1963, p. 11: 'The bulk of *Honest to God* has been written by a second Dr Robinson who is probably heretical and usually (unlike the orthodox Dr Robinson) muddled'; A. MacIntyre, 'God and the Theologians', in *The Honest to God Debate* (ed. D. L. Edwards and J. A. T. Robinson), London: SCM Press, 1963, p. 215: 'What is striking about Dr Robinson's book is first and foremost that he is an atheist.'

[5] London: SCM Press, 1965.

[6] The following paragraphs purport to be nothing more than a bare outline of a period of some 175 years. A very adequate survey is provided by Alec R. Vidler's recent study, *The Church in an Age of Revolution: 1789 to the present day*, London: Penguin, 1961.

[7] A. Vidler, *op. cit.*, p. 48.

sciences, highlighted by Darwinism. In February of that same year
the symposium, *Essays and Reviews*, was published. It provoked the
greatest religious crisis in nineteenth-century England. Basically,
the authors sought to counteract what they considered to be a
dangerous theological complacency then prevailing in England.
More specifically, they sought to bring English theology abreast of
the corresponding advances made in Germany over the past fifty
years. The reaction to the volume was swift and sharp. Controversy
raged for four or five years and then again, violently, in 1869.The
striking parallel with the current theological stirrings in England
should not be lost.[8]

In the 1880's English theology was still at a low ebb, not having
fully recovered from its negative and panic-stricken reaction to
Darwinism and to *Essays and Reviews*. The tide began to turn,
however, in 1889 with the publication of *Lux Mundi*, of which it has
been said that 'few books in modern times have so clearly marked
the presence of a new era and so deeply influenced its character'.[9]
It marked the definite emergence in the Church of England of
what Gore was fond of calling 'a liberal Catholicism'. Gore himself
hesitated to go beyond the new frontier marked out by *Lux Mundi*,
but in 1912 a younger group of Oxford scholars issued their own
contribution entitled, *Foundations: a Statement of Christian Belief in
Terms of Modern Thought*. The authors were following lines suggested
by certain of the Catholic Modernists and their ideas found common
expression in still another symposium, *Essays Catholic and Critical*, in
1926. This was indeed the high tide of liberal theology in England
and its spirit was to be reflected later in the Report to the Archbishop of Canterbury, *Doctrine in the Church of England*, in 1938. The
Commission had been appointed in 1922 but by the time it sub-
mitted its report, theological liberalism was beginning to ebb on the
Continent and Archbishop Temple in his introduction to the
report admitted that, if it were beginning its work again, 'its perspective would be different'.[10]

Just as English theology had been slow to respond to the challenge

[8] Bishop Robinson himself has noted this parallel in *The New Reformation?*, p. 12.
[9] Cited by Vidler, *The Church* . . . , p. 190.
[10] Cited by Vidler, *op. cit.*, p. 200.

of the new philosophical and theological movements in the nineteenth century, so, too, have the Continental developments in this
century been slow to take root. 'New ideas have always to be
anglicized before they can take root,' Bishop Robinson has remarked.
'As a result much of the doctrinal discussion that has taken place
has been in a vacuum. This is not to belittle the merit of the work
superbly summarized in Archbishop Ramsey's *From Gore to Temple*,[11]
only to say that it represents a closed and insular chapter which
takes little account of the continental ferment.'[12]

A major exception to this rule is C. H. Dodd. Like Robinson,
Dodd did his academic teaching in Cambridge where, since the
Second World War, a distinctive movement is becoming established,
associated now with such works as *Soundings*[13] and *Objections to
Christian Belief*.[14] And there has been a concomitant revival of
philosophical theology, largely stimulated by the critique brought
to bear by the linguistic analysts on the validity and meaning of
religious language. And so Christianity in England is now being
described as in a state of ferment, on the verge perhaps of a 'new
reformation'. This is the post-liberal (or what some others might
prefer to call the *neo*-liberal) era in English theology. It is within
this particular historical context that we now proceed to a consideration of the life, background, and writings of Bishop John A. T.
Robinson.

BIOGRAPHICAL SUMMARY[15]

Born in 1919 at Canterbury, John Arthur Thomas Robinson was
the son and grandson of Canons of Canterbury. His father died

[11] *From Gore to Temple: The Development of Anglican Theology Between Lux Mundi
and the Second World War, 1889–1939*, London: Longmans, 1960. (USA ed.
entitled *An Era of Anglican Theology* . . ., Scribners.)

[12] 'Keeping in Touch with Theology', *Twentieth Century*, summer, 1963;
reprinted in pamphlet form, London: SCM Press, 1963, p. 6.

[13] *Soundings: Essays Concerning Christian Understanding* (ed. A. R. Vidler), Cambridge University Press, 1962.

[14] London: Constable, 1963 (with intro. by A. R. Vidler).

[15] Except where otherwise specifically indicated, the material contained in this
section is based on a personal interview with Bishop Robinson on December 29,
1964, in London.

when the future bishop was only nine but he inherited from his
father, through his mother, 'a breadth and a depth and a largeness
of spirit to which I owe more than I know or can say. "Thou hast
set my feet in a large room" was one of his favourite texts. And
there were two men who for him more than any others embodied
this, the authentic spirit of the Anglican Church: Frederick Dennison
Maurice and Phillips Brooks. . . . What a largeness of spirit was
there! How can we hope, in this silver age, to fill out the Gospel as
he did![16] Our words have shrivelled, we are too critically conditioned
and self-conscious. Nevertheless the Gospel of the height, breadth,
length and depth of Christ remains as measureless as ever.'[17]
Robinson was educated at Jesus and Trinity Colleges, Cambridge,
where he read Classics, and the Philosophy of Religion. Prior to
ordination in 1945. He was at Westcott House Theological College.
He obtained his Ph.D in 1946 for a dissertation entitled, *Thou Who
Art: The notion of personality and its relation to Christian theology with
particular reference to* (a) *the contemporary 'I–Thou'philosophy;* (b) *the
doctrines of the Trinity and the Person of Christ.*[18] It was at this time,
in connection with his doctoral thesis, that he first read Karl Barth
and St Thomas Aquinas. He was especially sympathetic with Emil
Brunner's *The Divine–Human Encounter*[19] which adapted Martin
Buber's 'I–Thou' philosophy toChristianity.

Even though he had always intended to be ordained, Robinson
had begun reading the Classics at Cambridge.[20] Theology at the
time left much to be desired, in terms of relevance.[21] Reinhold

[16] He is referring to the collection of sermons, *The Candle of the Lord*, by Phillips
Brooks.

[17] 'Ascendancy', a sermon preached in Trinity Church, Boston, May 3, 1964,
and reprinted in the *Andover Newton Quarterly* n.s. 5 (1964) 5.

[18] Cambridge University, 1945 (unpublished).

[19] Republished as Part 2 of *Truth as Encounter* (tr. A. W. Loos and D. Cairns),
London: SCM Press, 1964.

[20] It is interesting to note that at least two other prominent English New
Testament scholars entered the field of Sacred Scripture through the same
academic door; namely, C. H. Dodd and C. F. D. Moule, both of whom were
to have a very significant influence on Bishop Robinson's New Testament
scholarship.

[21] Cf. his plea for a genuinely 'lay theology' in *The New Reformation?*, chapter 3,
pp. 54–77.

Niebuhr's provocative Gifford Lectures in 1939[22] were not at all typical of the contemporary English theological scene. Niebuhr had demonstrated, to Robinson at any rate, that the questions that theology asks must be relevant. Indeed, to shift the image slightly, it must be – to use Tillich's phrase – an 'answering theology',[23] attuned to the restless spirit of its own age.

After the Classics Robinson began reading in the Philosophy of Religion, having earlier developed an interest in philosophical theology. At this time certain of the great theological and philosophical classics were being translated into English, and so Robinson came under the influence of Berdyaev, Kierkegaard, and Buber. He also read most of William Temple's writings and attended some of C. H. Dodd's New Testament lectures. But it was through his doctoral dissertation that Robinson came into Theology from Philosophy – and it was a very gradual process. The thesis itself had brought him into a border-line area, somewhere between the two. Then, after a very brief pre-ordination theological course, he entered the ministry of the Church of England in 1945.

After Cambridge, Robinson spent three years as a curate at the Church of St Matthew, Moorfields, Bristol. The vicar at the time was Mervyn Stockwood, now Bishop of Southwark, under whom John A. T. Robinson is suffragan bishop of Woolwich. Stockwood was both pragmatic and progressive. The Parish Communion had the central place and the political and economic consequences of the liturgy were adeptly dramatized. Robinson's concern for socio-economic and political questions was intensified during his three years in this industrial parish. It is a concern that has not faded with the years;[24] indeed, it is evident even in some of his more scholarly works.[25] His most recent emphasis on the Church as a *secular community*, i.e. existing *for* the world, can be seen as a logical

---

[22] *The Nature and Destiny of Man* (2 vols.), New York: Scribner's Son, 1941 and 1943.

[23] Cf. *The New Reformation?*, p. 72.

[24] Cf. the various essays and addresses contained in *On Being the Church in the World*, London: SCM Press, 1960; cf. also his article, 'Five Points for Christian Action', in *Man and Society* 2 (1962) 13–15.

[25] It is particularly true of the 'Introduction' to *The Body*, London: SCM Press, 1952, pp. 7–10.

development from this earlier period.[26] His essay, 'The Social Content of Salvation', was a product of his curacy in Bristol, but it was not until 1952 that it was first published.[27]

In 1948 Robinson became chaplain and lecturer at Wells Theological College in Somerset. It was an Anglican seminary that was hardly affected by the various theological currents then at work on the Continent. Here he was asked to lecture on doctrine and on ethics. The latter course was primarily a study of current social questions, and in this he found the writings of Emil Brunner again very useful, as well as the highly personalist orientation of Buber, H. H. Farmer, and John Macmurray.[28] Subsequently, he was asked to lecture in the New Testament and, because he had done some work in the Gospels but none in St Paul while at Cambridge, he decided to lecture on the Epistles. From these lectures he would produce his important study of Pauline theology, *The Body*. His other monograph from this period was *In the End, God . . .*,[29] a book that was written from a doctrinal rather than a New Testament point of view – simply because his New Testament foundation was still in a very immature state. His interest had been primarily philosophical rather than theological or biblical, and it was from this point of view – philosophical rather than theological – that he was to review the recent French translation of Oscar Cullmann's *Christ*

[26] Cf. *The New Reformation?* where the theme of the 'servant-Church' is clearly delineated.

[27] *Frontier*, November, 1952; reprinted in *On Being the Church in the World*, pp. 23–30. Note the repetition of this theme in the 'Introduction' to *The Body*, p. 8: 'The content of social salvation for the modern man is to discover himself as a person, as one who freely chooses interdependence because his nature is to be made for others, rather than as one who is engulfed in it because the pressures of his age demand it. The alternative to the "They" is not the "I" but the "We".'

Another article was also published in this post-ordination period: 'The Temptations', *Theology* 50 (1947) 43–48; reprinted in *Twelve New Testament Studies*, London: SCM Press, 1962, pp. 53–60.

[28] Cf. *Honest to God* for the various references.

[29] London: James Clarke, 1950. *In The End, God . . .* contained some material that Robinson had published the year before: 'Universalism – Is it Heretical?' *Scottish Journal of Theology* 2 (1949) 139–155; cf. the rejoinder by T. F. Torrance, 'Universalism or Election?' in the same volume, pp. 310–318. (A revised edition of *In The End, God . . .* is due to appear in the series *Perspectives in Humanism*, New York: Harper & Row, 1967.)

and Time.[30] Indeed, in these early years he found Cullmann 'very sympathetic', 'the most Anglican in his ethos among the Continentals'. Cullmann's influence is especially evident in *The Body* and in a later article, 'The One Baptism'.[31]

One other item relevant to his stay at Wells should also be mentioned at this time, particularly because it, too, seemed to foreshadow what was yet to come in Robinson's academic and, later, episcopal career. On November 17, 1949, he delivered an address at the college on 'The House Church and the Parish Church'.[32] For the time, and certainly for the place, it had radical overtones, and the reaction to it was not uniformly favourable, to say the least.

In 1951 he became Fellow and Dean of Chapel at Clare College, Cambridge, succeeding C. F. D. Moule who continued to reside at the college. The two became very close friends. Moule, who like Robinson had come to New Testament studies by way of the Classics, was a man who commanded serious academic respect and his influence on Robinson should not be underestimated. It was here, then, in this highly stimulating atmosphere of Cambridge that Robinson completed work on *The Body* and wrote various articles and reviews.[33]

As a student at Cambridge Robinson had regarded Liturgy as one of the most irrelevant subjects in the entire curriculum. After ordination as a curate in Bristol he received an entirely new vision of the Parish Communion. And now, as Dean of Clare College, he found himself for the first time with full responsibility for a worshipping community. Here, too, for the first time, he was to see the

---

[30] *Scottish Journal of Theology* 3 (1950) 86–89.

[31] *Scottish Journal of Theology* 6 (1953) 257–274; reprinted in *Twelve New Testament Studies*, pp. 158–175.

[32] Reprinted in *On Being the Church in the World*, pp. 83–95.

[33] For example: 'The Theological College in a Changing World,' *Theology* 55 (1952) 202–207; 'Traces of a Liturgical Sequence in 1 Cor. xvi. 20–24,' *Journal of Theological Studies* n.s. 4 (1953) 38–41; 'The One Baptism,' *op. cit.*; 'The Christian Hope' in *Christian Faith and Communist Faith* (ed. D. M. Mackinnon), London: Macmillan, 1953, pp. 209–226; a review of J. Marsh's *The Fulness of Time*, in *Theology* 56 (1953) 107–109; and a significant review of Bultmann's newly translated *Theology of the New Testament*, 'The Hard-Core of the Gospel: New Thought from Germany', *The Church of England Newspaper*, February 27, 1953.

essential connection between the liturgy and evangelism. The question he had to face was this: 'How was the local Church – in this case the Christians in a college of about four hundred young men – to become effective as *the witnessing Community*, as the embodiment of the Gospel in action, placarding by its very being and structure the new life by which it lived?'[34] Robinson was convinced that the liturgical life as it was then constituted at Clare was hardly a 'working-model of the Gospel', and so he gave priority to liturgical reform – reform not so much of what was *said* but of what was *done*. 'The whole basis of what we sought to do was that every Christian in the College, whatever tradition or denomination he might belong to, whatever other religious organization he might or might not join, was before anything else a member of the Church of God as it found its local expression in Clare.' He felt that the chapel of an Anglican university should be faithful to the ideal of 'the complete Church of England man, abjuring party extremism (and at the same time any watery *via media*), stressing the things that unite rather than the things that divide'.[35]

By 1954 he had devised a New Communion Manual[36] to counteract what he regarded as the individualism, pietism, and subjectivism of the traditional 'catholic' and 'evangelical' manuals, both of which he found to be too clerical as well. The new manual, he felt, would 'genuinely represent the corporate understanding of the Eucharist which we had come to share'. And he discovered an appropriate language of theology and devotion 'mainly by a return to the Bible and the early liturgies, whose theology of the Body of Christ in relation both to the Church and the Sacrament, ante-dates the medieval divisions and distortions to which we are all heirs'.[37]

Robinson accepted a lectureship at Cambridge in 1953, which he held until his departure from the university in 1959. His first subject was the Epistle to the Romans, but he also lectured on the Theology and Ethics of the Gospels. Actually he had almost selected the Philosophy of Religion as his field, and this would not have been surprising in view of his earlier academic career as a student at Cambridge. However, he opted for New Testament and

---

[34] *Liturgy Coming to Life*, p. 10.
[36] *Ibid.*, pp. 77–109 (Part III).
[35] *Ibid.*, pp. 12–13.
[37] *Ibid.*, pp. 16–17.

from then until his appointment as Bishop of Woolwich, Robinson devoted himself entirely to New Testament studies. In 1955 he became a Visiting Professor at Harvard University, delivering the William Belden Noble lectures in December of that same year. The substance of these lectures was incorporated into another monograph appearing in 1957, *Jesus and His Coming*.[38] After completing his research and writing for this particular study, Robinson developed a very strong interest in the Johannine writings (on which he subsequently lectured in place of his course on the Theology and Ethics of the Gospels). This new interest is reflected in many of the contributions to his *Twelve New Testament Studies*[39] and other articles.[40] On the side, as it were, while lecturing along more academic lines at Cambridge, he also produced a collection of essays and addresses, *On Being the Church in the World*,[41] and *Liturgy Coming to Life*. He also produced a very significant contribution to the symposium, *The Historic Episcopate in the Fullness of the Church*.[42] A second visit to the United States in 1958 included the Reinecker Lectures at Virginia Theological Seminary. He was also one of the translators for the *New English Bible*, being a member of the New Testament Panel.

In 1959 Robinson became bishop of Woolwich in South-east London, as suffragan to his former vicar in Bristol, Mervyn Stockwood, now Bishop of Southwark. The decision was not an easy one

[38] London: SCM Press, 1957; Robinson's indebtedness to C. F. D. Moule is expressed in the preface, p. 7: ' . . . to whose forbearance and patient criticism almost every idea in this book has been subjected in the course of its development'.

[39] For example: 'The "Others" of John 4.38' (chapter IV); 'The Parable of the Shepherd (John 10.1–5)' (chapter V); 'The New Look on the Fourth Gospel' (chapter VII); 'The Destination and Purpose of St John's Gospel' (chapter VIII); 'The Destination and Purpose of the Johannine Epistles' (chapter IX).

[40] Cf. 'The Relation of the Prologue to the Gospel of John,' *New Testament Studies* 9 (1962) 120–129; 'The Significance of the Foot-Washing,' in *Neotestamentica et Patristica*, Leiden: Brill, 1962, pp. 144–147; and 'The Place of the Fourth Gospel,' in *The Roads Converge* (ed. P. Gardner-Smith), London: Arnold, 1963, pp. 49–74.

[41] 'They were written, with one early exception, at a time when my prime responsibility was the study and teaching of the New Testament. But they all represent "applied" rather than "pure" biblical theology' (preface, p. 7).

[42] 'Kingdom, Church and Ministry', in *The Historic Episcopate* (ed. K. M. Carey), London: Dacre Press, 1954 (2nd ed., 1960), pp. 11–22.

and he accepted only after five months' deliberation. He knew that it would entail a curtailment, if not a complete termination, of the scholarly endeavours in which he had been involved at Cambridge. He was gathering material on the origin and history of the Johannine tradition. There were other projects he had hoped to complete. For example, he would like to have combined the themes of *The Body* (our coming *into* Christ) and of *Jesus and His Coming* (the coming *of* Christ) and thereby to have considered our coming *together* in him. In the end, he chose to leave Cambridge for Woolwich because he had always seemed to thrive in a task that combined theology and practice rather than in a purely academic environment. In Woolwich he would confront a 'run-down ecclesiastical machine' over against a highly secularized society. It is within the context of this new challenge that his subsequent writings should be viewed. It would be totally incorrect to assume that the change in direction and tone in his post-Cambridge writings reflects a sudden disillusionment with biblical studies or the positive theological sciences, or further, that it is indicative of a fundamental change in theological perspective. Such a change would indeed have been remarkably radical – and equally inexplicable – since, as a New Testament scholar, he was noted for views that were generally conservative. He was not at all in the liberal Bultmannian tradition.[43] Furthermore, the pectoral cross presented to him by the undergraduates of Clare College still represents pictorially for him something of central theological importance.[44] The obverse side bears the figure of Christ, crucified, between the letters Alpha and Omega; the reverse side contains, in the centre, the ecumenical symbol of the World Council of Churches representing our unity in Christ today; underneath it there is a fish-symbol depicting our link through

---

[43] Cf., for example, the articles cited in footnotes 39 and 40, above. Cf. also his review of Bultmann's *Theology of the New Testament*, in *The Church of England Newspaper* and *Honest to God* (written ten years later), pp. 34–35. Robinson has even been accused of following a path of biblical research that belongs for the most part to a 'precritical age': cf. S. M. Gilmour, *Journal of Biblical Literature* 81 (1962) 427.

[44] In a letter to me, dated September 24, 1964, he wrote: 'The two sides of this sum up pictorially a good many of the things that seem to me central.'

the ages with the primitive Church; and, on either side, the loaf and the cup we share at Communion.[45]

Among his writings emanating from this new situation are a series of Advent addresses published in booklet form, *Christ Comes In*.[46] It presents some of the material from *Jesus and His Coming* in more easily digestible form and contains elements of a 'Son of Man' or 'man-for-others' Christology that would be reflected more fully in *Honest to God* and especially *The New Reformation?* He also contributed to another symposium on the episcopacy, *Bishops: What they are and what they do*; his own essay was entitled, 'A New Model of the Episcopacy', and was written in the light of his own episcopal experience, unlike his earlier contribution to *The Historic Episcopate*.[47] Serious academic material continued to appear as well, although the greater portion of it could be traced back to the Cambridge period.[48] His abiding interest in issues of practical import, evident during his years in Bristol and even during his stay at Cambridge,[49] was further manifested in a number of minor writings; for example, 'Five Points for Christian Action' in *Man and Society*, *The Church of England and Intercommunion* (a Prism pamphlet),[50] 'The Great Benefice Barrier',[51] 'The Ministry and the Laity' in *Layman's Church*,[52] 'The Tercentenary of the Book of Common Prayer' in *Parish and People*,[53] and a particularly important address to which we have already

[45] The reverse side of the cross is the cover design for the second edition (1963) of *Liturgy Coming to Life*. The explanation is found on p. xii.

[46] London: A. R. Mowbray, 1960.

[47] *Bishops: What they are and what they do* (ed. the Bishop of Llandaff), London: Faith Press, 1961, pp. 125–138.

[48] *Twelve New Testament Studies;* 'The Relation of the Prologue to the Gospel of John', *op. cit.;* 'Resurrection in the New Testament', *The Interpreter's Dictionary of the Bible*, New York: Abingdon Press, 1962, pp. 43–53 (vol. IV); 'The Significance of the Foot-Washing', *op. cit.;* and 'The Place of the Fourth Gospel', *op. cit.* This last article was written during the same period of convalescence as *Honest to God*.

[49] Cf., for example, *On Being the Church in the World* and *Liturgy Coming to Life*. Robinson has always been concerned with the problems of the Church in an industrial and urban society.

[50] London, 1962 (no. 2).

[51] *Prism*, no. 80 (December, 1963) 4–13.

[52] London: Lutterworth Press, 1963, pp. 9–22.

[53] Epiphany, 1963, no. 36, pp. 15–19.

referred in the Preface, 'The World that God Loves'. It was at this juncture that *Honest to God* appeared on the scene.

Honest to God gathered up various elements that were under the surface for many years. Robinson had first read Bonhoeffer, for example, in 1952 when the *Ecumenical Review* published certain extracts from the *Letters and Papers from Prison*.[54] He referred to Bonhoeffer's ideas now and then in the course of a sermon, but he never actually read him through until ten years later when sickness curtailed his active life for three months. He had already read Bultmann, but only in connection with his New Testament studies at Cambridge. He recognized the challenging character of Bultmann's essay, 'New Testament and Mythology', when he first read it in English translation in 1953, but was 'astonished to discover how Bultmann's ideas, for all their forbidding jargon, seemed to come like a breath of fresh air to entirely untheological students'.[55] Tillich's collection of sermons, *The Shaking of the Foundations*, first appeared in England in 1949. One of the sermons, 'The Depth of Existence', had an unusually strong impact upon him, opening his eyes to 'the transformation that seemed to come over so much of the traditional religious symbolism when it was transposed from the heights to the depths'.[56] Robinson was teaching at Wells Theological College at the time and he simply read Tillich's sermon to his students, in place of an address of his own. 'I do not remember looking at the words again till I came to write this, but they formed one of the streams below the surface that were to collect into the underground river of which I have since become conscious.'[57] The river was indeed 'underground' during the Cambridge period when New Testament studies occupied Robinson's primary attention. During a subsequent visit to Harvard, however, he met Tillich and was impressed by him, although he had always remained critical of Tillich's insufficient regard for the historical element of the New Testament. Robinson was later forced to confront Tillich's *Systematic Theology*[58] when preparing his own doctrinal lectures for the South-

[54] London: Collins, 1959; first published in English by SCM Press, 1953.
[55] *Honest to God*, p. 25.
[56] *Honest to God*, pp. 21–22.   [57] *Ibid.*, p. 22.
[58] London: Nisbet (3 vols.) 1953, 1957, 1965 (also Chicago: University Press).

wark Ordination Course for the training of priest-workers and others, of which he was the chief architect.

If there was any originality, then, in his now-famous *Honest to God*, it was, as we have already indicated, in bringing together these divergent streams of thought into a new synthesis and context. And this motive was essentially pastoral: 'It belongs to the office of a bishop in the Church to be a guardian and defender of its doctrine. I find myself a bishop at a moment when the discharge of this burden can seldom have demanded greater depth of divinity and quality of discernment.'[59] Its immediate source was the impact of the question that had always pressed upon him: 'How does the Church make any inroad at all in our industrial, secular civilization?' And it was really addressed to the sort of people that he had known at Cambridge.

As for his most recent book, *The New Reformation?*, which is much more pertinent to our understanding of Robinson's concept of the Church, this takes up where *Honest to God* left off. And so *The New Reformation?* asks the next question: 'So what for the Church?' 'How must the Church adapt her structures, her mission, and her life to the new situation which secularization poses for her?'

In between the publication of *Honest to God* and *The New Reformation?*, Robinson contributed to *The Honest to God Debate*.[60] In 1964 his pamphlet *Christian Morals Today*[61] appeared, based on three lectures in Liverpool Cathedral late in the preceding year. While Robinson's views on moral theology will not occupy much, if any, of our attention in this study, it is sufficient to note that Robinson himself admits to being 'most Protestant' in this general area. In addition to a paper to a consultation on religious television on 'Communicating with the Contemporary Man'[62] and numerous articles for popular papers, he has also written a brief study of

[59] *Honest to God*, p. 7.

[60] London: SCM Press, 1963, chapter 9, 'The Debate Continues', pp. 232–275. The reviews all appeared within three months of the publication of *Honest to God*. In Robinson's opinion, later reviews and comments exhibited more thought and maturity.

[61] London, SCM Press, 1964.

[62] *Religion in Television*, London: Independent Television Authority, 1964, pp. 27–35.

C. H. Dodd, in the 'Theologians of our Time' series of the *Expository Times*.[63] He also made a fourth visit to the United States in 1964 for a series of talks, including the Purdy Lectures at the Hartford Theological Seminary in Connecticut and the Thorpe Lectures at Cornell University at Ithaca, New York. His topic was *The New Reformation?*

We might conclude this biographical summary with a statement by the bishop which, although referring specifically to *Honest to God*, can serve as a guide-line or norm of interpretation for what has gone before as well as for what might yet lie ahead: 'Indeed my book was born of the fact that I knew myself to be a man committed without reservation to Christ *and* a man committed, without possibility of return, to modern twentieth-century secular society. It was written out of the belief that both these convictions must be taken with equal seriousness and that they *cannot* be incompatible.'[64]

THE ANGLICAN CONTEXT

We have thus far indicated by means of a general and, indeed, a superficial survey of the recent history of theology in Great Britain something of the tradition in which John A. T. Robinson has been formed. Our survey would be far from complete, however, were we to ignore the specifically Anglican heritage that is his. This is particularly important when the problem at hand is a proper evaluation of his ecclesiological perspective. For the author of *Honest to God* is also the author of *The Body*, and the Anglican Bishop of Woolwich besides. Anglicanism is indeed in his blood, as he has described it. But it is an Anglicanism without denominationalism, without serious concern for self-identification within the well-known strata of Anglican ecclesiastical polity: High Church or Low Church, Anglo-Catholic or Evangelical, or simply Broad Church. His is the 'most typical spirit of Anglicanism'[65]: the spirit of comprehensiveness. He has been critical of both Anglo-Catholics

[63] Reprinted in *Theologians of our Time* (joint eds. A. W. and E. Hastings), Edinburgh: T. & T. Clark, 1966, pp. 40-46.
[64] *Honest to God Debate*, p. 275.
[65] W. H. Van de Pol, *The Christian Dilemma*, London: Dent, 1952, p. 203.

and Liberals, particularly with regard to the debate on church
unity in which they were both engaged between the two world wars.
The Anglo-Catholics, he has suggested, placed far too much
emphasis on the ministry and apostolic succession: no bishop, no
Church! Any doctrine of the Kingdom, i.e. of God's universal rule
in history, was subordinated to his design for his Church, and issues
in the contemporary world did not sufficiently concern them. The
Liberals, on the other hand, appeared to emphasize the *Kingdom*
rather than the Kingdom *of God*. They maintained too low a
doctrine of the Church, subordinating it to the Social Gospel or the
religious experience of the individual; and so, too, was their doctrine
of the ministry inadequate. The views of the Anglo-Catholics pre-
vailed, aided partly by the strength of their principles and partly by
the direction of world events. Thus, the question of the Church of
South India, for example, was debated almost entirely on the
Anglo-Catholic priority: 'The Church must be judged by the
Ministry, and the Kingdom by the Church.'

'In this rather depressing situation', he wrote, 'the most significant
new factor has been the revival in biblical theology, of which in this
field the Bishop of Durham's *The Gospel and the Catholic Church*[66]
was the harbinger. The result of this revival has been to confirm the
position of neither party. Its most immediate and obvious consequence was to confound the Liberals. It convicted them of having
pitched their doctrine alike of the Kingdom, the Church and the
Ministry too low. . . . But of greater significance in the long run
will perhaps be the question which this biblical theology has put
against the whole Anglo-Catholic sequence of priorities.

'The renewed interest in the theology of the New Testament has
revealed indeed that nothing less than the highest doctrine of the
ministry is compatible with the teaching and practice of Apostolic
Christianity . . . providing always our doctrine of the Church is
higher. But it does not stop there. For as the ministry is a function
of the Church, so the Church is a function of the Kingdom, of the
universal Lordship of God in Christ.'[67]

[66] A. M. Ramsey, London: Longmans, 1936; 2nd ed., 1956. Ramsey is now
Archbishop of Canterbury.
[67] 'Kingdom, Church, and Ministry', *op. cit.*, pp. 12–15.

Robinson's strong disavowal of Anglo-Catholicism must be read in the light of the preceding material and with an eye to his further remark that 'it is impossible to be a biblical theologian without being a high Churchman'.[68] But it is a newer type of high church-manship that is at issue, one that has 'emerged from the revival of biblical theology and the liturgical movement, and which really is concerned with a high doctrine of the Church as the Body of Christ, (but also) one that is equally at home in "evangelical" as in "catholic" circles'.[69]

Recently, however, he has become more and more impatient with the High Church group as its interests persist in being Church-centred rather than Kingdom-centred. 'The ecumenical venture will keep its vision and its course only if it has a higher doctrine of the Church than it does of the Ministry and a higher doctrine of the Kingdom than it does of the Church. Reverse these priorities, as so much "Church-bound" debate does, and how sterile it becomes! If we are a "bridge-Church" in the sense of being a bridge merely from Church to Church, and not from the world to the Kingdom, we shall find, as we are already in danger of finding, that no-one will want to walk on us.'[70]

Late in 1960 the *Christian Century* published an article by Bishop James A. Pike, of the Episcopal Diocese of California, in which he described how his thinking had changed over the previous ten years.[71] The title of the article, 'Three-Pronged Synthesis', suggested that the landmarks by which he was measuring this change were the traditional divisions of Anglican ecclesiology: High Church, Low Church, and Broad Church. Bishop Pike's article is important for our purposes because Bishop Robinson has indicated that it is a generally accurate account of his own growth and development.[72] Pike – and Robinson – finds that he is now more 'broad church', i.e. more liberal in theology, seeing his earlier neo-orthodox theology as entirely too vertical. He is willing to see more truth and goodness

[68] *On Being the Church in the World*, p. 16.
[69] *Liturgy Coming to Life*, p. 13.
[70] *The World that God Loves*, p. 5.
[71] *The Christian Century* 77 (1960), 1496–1500; reprinted in *Pacific Churchman* 97 (1961), 10–11, 19–20.
[72] Interview, December 29, 1964; cf. also *Honest to God*, p. 20.

in natural man who finds himself outside the Christian community and to see more value in agnosticism and atheism, for we must all be prepared to debunk the 'small god' and admit that we 'don't know' many things about theology. 'In short', Pike wrote, 'I don't believe as many things as I believed ten years ago. But I trust that what I do believe, I believe more deeply.'[73]

Secondly, Bishop Pike claimed to be more 'low church', more willing to learn from others and to adapt, less inclined to give 'final status' to particular forms of the Church. 'To me, "low church", in the sense of evangelical, is to believe that the Church is beyond any particular national churches, beyond particular denominations, beyond particular forms and traditions, beyond particular doctrinal formulations.'[74] And, finally, he admits to being more 'high church' with regard to the liturgy and the episcopacy in particular. The latter he regards to be of the *plene esse* of the Church. In summary: '(1) I am more broad church, that is, I know less than I used to think I knew; I have become in a measure a "liberal" in theology. (2) I am more low church, in that I cannot view divided and particular denominations as paramount in terms of the end-view of Christ's Church, and I do regard the Gospel as the all-important and as the *only final* thing. And (3) I am more high church, in that I more value the forms of the continuous life of the catholic church as best meeting the needs of people and best expressing the unity of Christ's church. These forms include liturgical expression and the episcopate.'[75]

The preceding pages have been designed to set Bishop John A. T. Robinson – the man and his theology – within the context of the contemporary theological situation. Various theological themes and questions have merely been alluded to in one connection or another. In the following chapters we intend to isolate – to the extent that such isolation is possible – the major ecclesiological elements in his thought and writings, and to subject them to careful analysis and criticism. What we have thus far merely suggested, we now intend to explore in greater detail.

[73] *Christian Century* 77 (1960), 1498.
[74] *Ibid.*, p. 1499.
[75] *Ibid.*, p. 1500.

Part One

THE NATURE OF THE CHURCH

2

THE CHURCH:
THE BODY OF CHRIST

WITH a consideration of the Church as the 'Body of Christ', one touches upon the deepest and innermost reality of her nature. The question is sometimes posed whether the notion of 'People of God' *or* that of the 'Body of Christ' is more central in New Testament ecclesiology. However, as R. Schnackenburg has correctly suggested, 'Anyone who has studied the documents of the New Testament and their theology attentively enough, will substitute an "and" in place of the "or".'[1] The Church in the New Testament is indeed the new 'People of God', but a people newly constituted in Christ and upon Christ, as its Head, its foundation, the source of its life and growth, and its final term. Admittedly, there is always a danger in emphasizing the notion of the Body at the expense of the notion of the 'People of God', with its peculiarly dynamic, historical character, and, in this event, one runs the risk of viewing the Church too abstractly and too speculatively. A balance must properly be maintained, for 'the Church is the People of God insofar as it is the Body of Christ, and it is the Body of Christ in a sense determined by the notion of the People of God, which serves as its foundation'.[2]

[1] *Die Kirche im Neuen Testament: Ihre Wirklichkeit und theologische Deutung, Ihr Wesen und Geheimnis*, Freiburg-im-Breisgau: Herder, 1961, p. 146 [Engl. *The Church in the New Testament* (tr. W. J. O'Hara), New York: Herder, 1965]; cf. also A. Oepke, 'Leib Christi oder Volk Gottes bei Paulus?', *Theologische Literaturzeitung* 79 (1954) 363–368; cf. also Y. Congar, 'The Church: The People of God' (tr. K. Sullivan), *Concilium* 1 (1965) 7–19.

[2] R. Schnackenburg, *Die Kirche*, p. 147; cf. also Y. Congar, *Lay People in the Church* (tr. D. Attwater), Westminster, Md: Newman, 1957, p. 22.

Therefore, our initial consideration of the Church as the Body of Christ does not preclude this other side of the ecclesiological equation. While John A. T. Robinson does not specifically treat this particular biblical image of the Church as 'People of God' in any of his writings, one can hardly conclude that his view of the Church is truncated and – more ironically – juridical and/or abstract. On the contrary, as we shall see in the next chapter especially, his view of the Church as the 'eschatological community' incorporates this theology of the 'People of God' to the extent that he clearly sets the Body of Christ in the context of the history of salvation, on march and in pilgrimage.[3] The terminology is absent, but not the reality.

Our method will be similar to that employed in the preceding chapter; namely, a consideration of the state of the question (historical context); an exposition of Robinson's position as contained in *The Body: A Study in Pauline Theology*, but not exclusively there; and, finally, a critical evaluation, taking into account the reviews and analyses of other New Testament scholars, both Catholic and Protestant.

STATE OF THE QUESTION

'One could say without exaggeration', Robinson writes in his 'Introduction' to *The Body*, 'that the concept of the body forms the keystone of Paul's theology. . . . It is from the body of sin and death that we are delivered; it is through the body of Christ on the Cross that we are saved; it is into His body the Church that we are incorporated; it is by His body in the Eucharist that this Community is sustained; it is in our body that its new life has to be manifested; it is to a resurrection of this body to the likeness of his glorious body that we are destined.'[4]

As might have been expected, the last three decades have produced a wide variety of opinions on the meaning of the *soma Christou* in St Paul. The differences have existed not only *among* the exegetes

[3] Cf. The Second Vatican Council's *Dogmatic Constitution on The Church* (*Lumen Gentium*), chap. 7, 'The Eschatological Nature of the Pilgrim Church and its Union with the Church in Heaven'. (Promulgated during the third session, 21 November, 1964.)

[4] *Op. cit.*, p. 9.

but also – more recently – *between* exegetes and theologians. More accurate, perhaps, is the observation of Yves Congar: 'When one reads on one side the simple expositions of the theologians and, on the other, the subtle discussions of the exegetes, one often has the impression that each is working in his own area, without regard for the other's conclusions.'[5]

An adequate account of the state of the question, therefore, should embrace both the exegetical and the theological development as well. Given the limited scope of this book, it will be impossible to do more than offer a very brief survey of each area. The encyclical letter of Pope Pius XII, *Mystici Corporis*,[6] will provide a focal point for our discussion.

1. *Exegetical Development*

Prior to the appearance of *Mystici Corporis* in 1943, the consensus of opinion among Catholic exegetes and theologians was that the Pauline notion of the body of Christ (*soma Christou*) had an exclusively collective meaning.[7] The Church, in this view, was simply the *collegium Christianorum*. It was this general point of view that was endorsed and proclaimed in the encyclical letter of Pope Pius XII. Indeed, so widely accepted has been this understanding of the *soma Christou* in a collective sense, that T. Zapalena was able to characterize the contrary opinion – L. Cerfaux's specifically – as 'foreign to Catholic tradition, (and) out of harmony with the magisterium of the Church'.[8]

Among the proponents of the so-called 'traditional' opinion that flourished in the period prior to 1943 was F. Prat, whose two-volume *Theology of St Paul*[9] was a standard reference work for years

---

[5] 'Peut-on définir l'Eglise? Destin et valeur de quatre notions qui s'offrent à le faire,' in *Sainte Eglise: Etudes et approches ecclésiologiques*, Paris: Cerf, 1963, p. 30.

[6] *Acta Apostolicae Sedis* 35 (1943) 193–248.

[7] Cf. the excellent survey article by J. Havet, 'La doctrine paulinienne du "Corps du Christ", essai de mise au point', *Littérature et Théologie Pauliniennes* (*Recherches Bibliques*, vol. 5), Louvain: Desclée de Brouwer, 1960, pp. 185–216. On a more popular level, cf. C. F. Mooney, 'Paul's Vision of the Church in Ephesians,' *Scripture* 15 (1963) 33–43.

[8] 'Vos estis corpus Christi (I Cor. 12.17),' *Verbum Domini* 37 (1959) 168.

[9] *Theology of St Paul*, 2 vols. (tr. J. Stoddard), Westminster: Newman, 1927; cf. especially vol. 1, pp. 300–308, and vol. 2, pp. 285–288 and 297–299.

in Catholic seminaries and colleges. Prat's view has since been supplanted by that of L. Cerfaux,[10] P. Benoit[11] and others, including John A. T. Robinson. We shall return to the pertinent issues in our subsequent discussion of Bishop Robinson's position. It would be sufficient at this point simply to indicate the basic element in Cerfaux's exegesis that sets him off from the earler view.

A key text for the proper understanding of the Pauline concept of the *soma Christou* is I Cor. 12.12–13a: 'For Christ is like a single body with its many limbs and organs, which, many as they are, together make up one body. For indeed we were all brought into one body by baptism.' It is here, and particularly with regard to verse 13a, that Cerfaux makes his departure from the earlier exegesis: 'We agree with E. Percy, *Der Leib Christi*, pp. 9–46, in saying that the expression "the body of Christ", as applied to the community, has in mind the *physical* body of Christ.'[12] And further on: '. . . . we refuse to see in $\sigma\tilde{\omega}\mu\alpha$ the meaning of "social body". The Church is a body only by way of allusion to the principle of unity which is the body of Christ, and $\sigma\tilde{\omega}\mu\alpha$, without anything to which it is referred, and even more $\mathrm{\mathring{\iota}v}\ \sigma\tilde{\omega}\mu\alpha$, means a human body or the body of Christ, but always a *physical* person.'[13] Incorporation into the Church by baptism means incorporation into the real, risen body of Christ.

2. *Theological Development*

While the history of recent exegesis on the notion of the body of Christ spans but a few decades, we are dealing with centuries when we attempt to outline the comparable development in the area of ecclesiology. The development of Catholic ecclesiology from the period of the Counter-Reformation to our own day is a familiar story and there is no point in re-tracing it here.[14] It has progressed from an emphasis that has been juridical and jealous of papal

[10] *The Church in the Theology of St Paul* (tr. G. Webb and A. Walker), New York: Herder, 1959; cf. especially pp. 262–281 and 384–389.

[11] 'Corps, tête et plerôme dans les épîtres de la captivité,' *Revue Biblique* 63 (1956) 5–44.

[12] Cerfaux, *The Church in the Theology of St Paul*, p. 270, n. 15 (italics mine).

[13] *Ibid.*, p. 274 (italics mine).

[14] Cf., for example, Y. Congar, *Lay People in the Church* (tr. D. Attwater), Westminster: Newman, 1959, pp. 22–52.

authority (in the period of Robert Bellarmine, for example) through a period of renewal in the last century under the leadership of Johann Adam Möhler, into a few brief moments of extremism wherein the Church became identified with a spiritual community devoid, for all practical purposes, of an hierarchial or visible constitution to speak of. It was in this latter context that Pope Pius XII wrote his encyclical letter in 1943, to counteract this so-called 'false mysticism' of certain Continental (i.e. German) theologians.[15] In the process of refutation the Pope developed a theology of the Church that was constructed according to the *theological* tradition of the Latin Church that viewed the *soma Christou* in a corporative, collective sense, and in the light of the predominant *exegesis* of the time.[16] For *Mystici Corporis* the Church is a 'body' in a way analogous to the human body.[17] The Church is the Body of Christ because 'our Lord is the Founder, the Head, the Support and the Saviour of this Mystical Body'.[18] The interpretation of the key text I Cor. 12.13 is clearly corporative.[19] In fact, as Congar has observed,[20] the corporative understanding of the *soma Christou* is the foundation for all the encyclical's theology: our spiritual dependence upon Christ, the 'Christusmythik' of the exegetes, the 'gratia capitis' of the Scholastics, the theology of the sacraments, and the theology of the Holy Spirit.

It would be an exaggeration to say that both the theological tradition that we have outlined above and the recent exegetical consensus that seems to have developed are perfectly wedded in the dogmatic constitution, *Lumen Gentium* (*De Ecclesia*), of the Second Vatican Council. However, it does seem clear that the mutual influences have been exercised and felt and that the constitution moves beyond the boundaries of the encyclical.[21]

It is in the context of this account of the state of the question that we proceed to a consideration of John A. T. Robinson's understanding of the Church as the Body of Christ.

[15] *AAS* 35 (1943) 197.
[16] Cf. Y. Congar, 'Peut-on définir l'Eglise?' in *Sainte Eglise*, Paris: Cerf, 1963, p. 30. The encyclical gives evidence of very heavy reliance upon St Augustine, St Thomas Aquinas, and St Robert Bellarmine, whereas there are only occasional references to the writings of the great Eastern Fathers.
[17] *AAS* 35, p. 199.   [18] *Ibid.*, p. 204.   [19] *Ibid.*, pp. 202–203.
[20] 'Peut-on définir l'Eglise?' p. 30.   [21] Cf. chapter 1, paragraph 7.

THE 'BODY OF CHRIST'
ACCORDING TO BISHOP ROBINSON

Our principal, although by no means exclusive, source for the task of reconstructing the notion of the Body of Christ in Bishop Robinson's writings is *The Body: A Study in Pauline Theology*, first published in 1952 and a product of his years at Wells Theological College and the early months at Cambridge. The book is a work of exegesis and biblical theology, but the orientation is clearly pastoral. Although he does not refer to it explicitly, a previous article, 'The Social Content of Salvation'[22], is the source of most of the material developed in the 'Introduction'. A study of this article would enhance one's appreciation of the perspective – sociological as well as theological – with which the book was written.

Salvation, for Robinson, is historically conditioned in so far as the eternal life of God becomes incarnate in the historically conditioned lives of men and women on earth. 'This means', he observes, 'that, while the soul of salvation is eternally the same, its body is always changing. The particular ideal of life which in any age translates into a pattern of concrete social relationships the fulfilment of the human spirit in God requires to be redefined with every fundamental change in the structure of society. Salvation becomes disembodied, and therefore irrelevant (for it is through the body alone that men perceive the soul), when this redefinition is not made. And the fact that it has not yet been fully made in our generation lies at the root of the ineffectiveness of much present-day evangelism.'[23]

Robinson proceeds to define 'social salvation' as 'a position in society in which a man really finds himself, where he counts, is of value, and can make a difference'. And the 'content of social salvation' is 'what a man has to become in order to find fulfilment as a member of society'.[24] This will differ from society to society, and the Church must take these variations into account. With this in mind, he suggests a threefold division of the social relationship: pre-scientific society, capitalist society, and socialized society (not *socialist*, but *socialized* in the sense outlined by *Pacem in Terris*).[25]

[22] Reprinted in *On Being the Church in the World*, pp. 23–30.
[23] *On Being the Church in the World*, p. 23.
[24] *Ibid.*, pp. 23–24.   [25] *Ibid.*, p. 26, n. 1.

In the pre-scientific society man is dependent upon nature for his livelihood. *Dependence* is the controlling theme. It is a society that is hierarchically structured. Social salvation in this society consists in acquiring some function as a member, or limb, of the body politic, on which in turn the health of the whole depends. The Church offered salvation to this society by holding out to the individual the possibility of incorporation into an organism. 'For this reason', Robinson states, 'its gospel appeared relevant. It spoke to men of becoming members or limbs of a Body: it offered them value as functional parts of the *Corpus Christi*. It knew what salvation, if it were to have any appeal, must show men the way to become – not individuals (that was not yet the social ideal), but dependent members of a whole. For such incorporation mass conversion was the adopted technique and the "dependent" virtues of poverty, chastity . . . and obedience the ideal of perfection.'[26]

In the second stage and type of society, the capitalist form, the controlling theme and key idea is *independence*. In this society we have the power to control and manipulate nature for our own ends. Social salvation consists in becoming an individual, not in becoming a dependent member. 'Social salvation meant, as the novels of Dickens so clearly illustrate, the rescuing of men to become individuals out of the mass of the proletariat who had no "name" or identity, no power to count in society, because they had no capital.'[27] The Reformation, according to Robinson, spoke to this new society in relevant terms even though 'Protestantism defaulted disastrously in its gospel to society'.[28] And with this new ideal of salvation there developed inevitably an individualistic piety and ethic and 'on the radical wing of the Protestant movement, at any rate, the notion of a "gathered Church" and of congregational autonomy superseded the *Una Sancta* of Catholicism'.[29] With this change of goals there was a corresponding change in technique: from 'mass conversions' entailing incorporation in a Body to the concept of rescuing individual souls for whom Christ died.

In the third and, for Robinson, the current stage of social development, there is the socialized society – a synthesis of the first two

[26] *On Being the Church in the World*, pp. 24–25.
[28] *Ibid.*, p. 26.
[27] *Ibid.* p. 25.
[29] *Idem. loc. cit.*

types. Herein the key idea is *interdependence*. 'In place of the feudal thesis of slavish dependence and the capitalist antithesis of selfish independence, the ideal is of a freedom found in the reciprocity of community service.'[30] This ideal stage, however, remains threatened by a new form of tyranny which submerges the individual in the mass of society, with little value and no voice, swallowed up in impersonality. For him redemption means 'being released to become a person – not an individual, because in independence he is power- less in face of the all-controlling State – but a person, who may find rather than lose himself in the interdependence of the community'. And in tones that certainly echo the philosophy of Martin Buber: 'The "they" depersonalizes: a man achieves personality . . . when he discovers himself addressed and treated as a "thou" and can respond in the same way in his relationships to others. The content of social salvation for the modern man is to discover himself as a person, as one who freely chooses interdependence, because his nature is to be made for others, rather than one who is engulfed in it because the pressures of his age demand it.'[31] It is to this age and this new social situation that the Church must speak, demonstrating the possibilities of becoming truly a person through Christianity alone. Conversion must be both a personal and a community affair: 'For a man becomes a person when he discovers himself in the I–Thou relation of community and in actual experience grasps with the total response of his being that he has been made for, and has his centre in, other persons.'[32] It is in this sense that Robinson rejects both the medieval interpretation of the Church as the *Corpus Christi*, which precedes the individual and into which he is grafted, as well as the Protestant conception of the Church as the gathered con- gregation, which exists only as a result of an aggregation of indivi- duals.

The Body addresses itself to this new social situation which is characterized by the reality of interdependence, and springs from

---

[30] *On Being the Church in the World*, p. 27.　　　　[31] *Ibid.*, pp. 27–28.

[32] *Ibid.*, p. 28. One can see already anticipated in this article, itself a product of his curacy in Bristol (1946), themes that would later reappear in *Honest to God*, i.e. Christ as 'the man for others', and *The New Reformation?*, i.e. the Servant Church.

his conviction that 'in the Pauline concept of the body there is something of profound implication and relevance both for the understanding of this problem (which, it must be remembered, is nothing
less than *the* social, political and religious problem of our age) and
for its Christian solution'.[33] Paul starts from the fact that man is
bound up in 'a vast solidarity of historical existence which denies
him freedom to control his own destiny or achieve his true end', but
he avoids the 'temptation of Western man . . . to seek salvation by
exalting the individual *against* such collectives or by seeking with-
drawal from the body of socio-historical existence'. The body is not
something simply evil; solidarity is the 'divinely ordained structure
in which personal life is to be lived'. Our hope lies not in escape from
our social relationships but rather in the resurrection of the body, i.e.
'in the redemption, transfiguration, and ultimate supersession of one
solidarity by another'. This is the message of Paul. The concept of
the body forms the 'keystone' of his theology and is perhaps 'the
most striking mark of its *distinctiveness*'.[34]

Robinson has divided his treatment of the Pauline theology of the
body in a threefold manner: the Body of the Flesh (chapter I);
the Body of the Cross (chapter II); and the Body of the Resurrection
(chapter III). The concern of the first chapter is anthropological,
that of the second chapter is soteriological, and, finally, that of the
third chapter is ecclesiological. The outline and development is
logical enough and there is no reason to depart from this schema in
our exposition of Robinson's concept of the Body of Christ.

1. *Anthropological Notions*

Paul's anthropology is clearly Hebrew and the basic categories
with which he works derive from the Old Testament view of man.
Yet in the Old Testament there is no term as such which corresponds
to *soma*. The closest equivalent would be *basar* (flesh, *sarx*) and this
seems to be the common Hebrew original for 'flesh' and 'body' in

---

[33] *The Body*, p. 8.
[34] *Ibid.*, pp. 8–9; cf. also *In the End, God* . . . , especially chapter 7, pp. 83 ff.;
cf. also D. M. Stanley, 'Reflections on the Church in the New Testament,'
Catholic Biblical Quarterly 25 (1963) 387–400, esp. p. 395.

the Pauline writings. First of all, there is no opposition between matter and form in Hebrew thought and so *basar* would signify the whole life-substance of man or beasts as organized in corporeal form. Secondly, according to Robinson, there is no opposition between the one and the many in Hebrew thought and indeed almost any part can be used to represent the whole. Thirdly, there exists no anti-thesis between body and soul in the Old Testament anthropology. There is a question only of an animated body, and not an incarnated soul. And, fourthly, *soma* as opposed to *sarx* (σάρξ) is not the principle of individuation: 'True individuality was seen to be grounded solely in the indivisible responsibility of each man to God. . . . The flesh-body was not what partitioned a man off from his neighbour; it was rather what bound him in the bundle of life with all men and nature, so that he could never make his unique answer to God as an isolated individual, apart from his relation to his neighbour.'[35]

For Paul *sarx* is 'the whole person, considered from the point of view of his external, physical existence'.[36] *Sarx* suggests man in contrast with God, man in his weakness and mortality, man in his worldliness, in the solidarity of earthly existence. It is 'a relation of ambiguity to God, since the world to which he is bound in the flesh is a world fallen under sin and death'.[37] When Paul speaks of sin as living κατὰ σάρκα, he is not suggesting that there is some opposition between reason and the passions, but only that such an attitude entails a denial of the human situation over against God. *Sarx* can have either a neutral or a sinful connotation: in the former sense it refers to man as living *in* the world, and in the latter sense it refers to man as living *for* the world. He becomes a 'man of the world' by allowing his being-in-the-world to govern his whole life and conduct.

Paul's concept of the body (*soma*), on the other hand, is strikingly different from his notion of the flesh (*sarx*). *Soma* is the bridge between *sarx* and Paul's doctrine of man, Christ, the Church, and eternal life. Like *sarx*, *soma* also refers to the external man, i.e. the 'body' as it is commonly understood. It refers not only to something man *has*, but also to something that he *is*. Essentially the relationship between *sarx* and *soma* consists in the fact that they 'designate different aspects

---

[35] *The Body*, p. 15; cf. also *On Being the Church in the World*, pp. 31–42.
[36] *The Body*, pp. 17–18.   [37] *Ibid.*, p. 22.

of the human relationship to God. *While σάρξ stands for man, in the solidarity of creation, in his distance from God, σῶμα stands for man, in the solidarity of creation, as made for God.*'[38] This basic contrast is most clearly evident in I Cor. 6.13–20. 'The body is for the Lord;' but it is not sufficient for Paul merely to repeat that since he knows that the body of human life now belongs securely to the *sarx* and the powers of sin. He goes further and says that 'the Lord (is) for the body. God not only raised our Lord from the dead; he will also raise us by his power' (I Cor. 6.13–14). How this redemption and resurrection of the body is made possible is the subject of Robinson's second chapter.

2. *Soteriological Notions*

It is in Gal. 4.3–5 that Paul states the full import of his enigmatic phrase in I Cor. 6.13: ὁ κύριος τῷ σώματι, 'the Lord for the body'. The human situation into which 'God sent forth his Son' was one of death, of sin, and of subjection to the law. For the Hebrew, death is never a purely natural phenomenon, but rather 'the sacrament and symbol of defeat by death: physical expiration is the outward confirmation of being in fact already "dead" (νεκρός; Eph. 2.1)'.[39] Sin is 'the accomplice of death' and the human condition involves slavery to sin. Sin is a symbol now, not of freedom, but of determinism, of something that has got out of man's control. The law is the instrument of sin. As death comes through sin (Rom. 5.12), so sin comes 'through the law' (Rom. 7.5). The whole process and state of man's triple enslavement is portrayed in Rom. 7.11. It is 'a single interrelated complex of bondage and frustration'.[40]

In the Incarnation the Son of God identified himself, to the limit, yet without sin, with the body of the flesh in its fallen state. He took the form of a slave (Phil. 2.5–8) without being enslaved; he was 'made sin for us' (II Cor. 5.21) without being a sinner; and he 'became a curse for us' (Gal. 3.13) without being accursed. By his death on the Cross Christ defeated these forces and demonstrated their impotence. The death of Christ is the defeat of evil because death consists in liberation from the flesh. 'The Resurrection is the

---

[38] *The Body*, p. 31; cf. also especially pp. 31–32, n. 1.
[39] *Ibid.*, pp. 35–36.   [40] *Ibid.*, p. 37.

inevitable consequence of this defeat; death could have no grip on Him, since sin obtained no foothold in Him.'[41] For Christ death was both the symbol and the sacrament of his voluntary act of putting off the flesh. 'On that cross He discarded the cosmic powers and authorities like a garment; He made a public spectacle of them and led them as captives in His triumphal procession' (Col. 2.15). Death was his release from sin (Rom. 6.10; 8.3) and from the curse of the law (Gal. 3.13).

Christ's redemptive work on the Cross is reproduced in the life of the Christian through baptism, whereby he is released from the powers of death (Col. 2.20; Rom. 8.2), of sin (Rom. 6.6), and of the law (Rom. 7.4). 'The whole work of Christ in redemption can be summed up for Paul in the words: "You, being in time past alienated and enemies in your mind in your evil works, yet now hath he reconciled *in the body of his flesh through death*" (ἐν τῷ σώματι τῆς σαρκὸς αὐτοῦ διὰ τοῦ θανάτου: Col. 1.21 f.; *cf.* Eph. 2.15 f.).'[42] The relation of Christ and the Christian is not to be understood extrinsically, as a relationship of mere imitation. That is not Paul's doctrine of the Atonement. For him the nexus is not one of example but of something that can be expressed only by a variety of prepositions: *in, with, through, of, into* Christ.[43] The underlying assumption of these texts is central to Pauline soteriology: '*Christians have died in, with and through the crucified body of the Lord . . . because, and only because, they are now in and of His body in the "life that he liveth unto God", viz., the body of the Church.*'[44] It is through baptism that the Christian enters the one body (I Cor. 12.13) and it is through the Body of Christ that a man can be saved through the Body of the Cross (I Cor. 10.16). 'The Christian, because he is in the Church and united with Him in the sacraments, is part of Christ's body so literally that all that happened in and through that body in the flesh can be repeated in and through him now. This connection comes to clearest expression in Rom. 7.4: "Wherefore, my brethren, ye also were made dead to the law *through the body of Christ;* that ye should be joined to another, even to him who was raised from the dead."

[41] *The Body*, p. 40.
[42] *Ibid.*, p. 45.
[43] For the pertinent texts, cf. *The Body*, p. 46.   [44] *Ibid.*, p. 47.

Here the words in italics mean *both* "through the fact that Christ in His flesh-body died to the law" *and* "through the fact that you now are joined to and are part of that body".'[45]

The concept of the body, then, supplies the 'linch-pin' of Paul's thought and is his point of departure for his ecclesiology. 'Whatever the linguistic source or sources may have been from which Paul brought that most characteristic of all his expressions, τὸ σῶμα τοῦ Χριστοῦ, it should be axiomatic that it has to be elucidated and interpreted, not primarily in terms of these sources, but *in terms of his own Christology*.'[46]

3. Ecclesiological Notions

Bishop Robinson treats of Pauline ecclesiology under the heading, 'The Body of the Resurrection'. The title was deliberately chosen 'so as to bring together under a single treatment the Pauline doctrine of what is usually differentiated as the glorified, the mystical and the eucharistic body of Christ, along with the Christian's hope of the resurrection and renewal of his own body'.[47] The inextricable relatedness of all Paul's uses of *soma* has often been obscured by the very success of his description of the Church as the Body of Christ. The word 'body' ordinarily is used to refer to a group of people, a collectivity. But this meaning was quite unfamiliar, if not entirely unknown, to the people to whom Paul was writing. '(Paul) never speaks of "a body of Christians" but always of "the Body of Christ". For him, at any rate, the word clearly referred to the organism of a particular person.'[48] Hereafter Robinson clearly adopts the so-called 'realistic' exegesis of the *soma Christou*.

In his consideration of I Cor. 6.15, for example, he insists that Paul is referring not to a society but to a person, the person of the

---

[45] *Idem, loc. cit.*

[46] *Ibid.*, p. 48; cf. also *In the End, God* . . ., pp. 83–98; 'Resurrection in the NT', *The Interpreter's Dictionary of the Bible*, vol. 4, p. 52; 'Cur Present Position in the Light of the Bible,' in *Becoming a Christian* (ed. B. Minchin), London: Faith Press, 1954, pp. 48–57, where Robinson considers the sacrament of baptism in the light of the organic life of the Body of Christ; for the appreciation of the centrality of the Body of Christ alongside the Parousia-event, cf. *Jesus and His Coming*, p. 184.

[47] *The Body*, p. 49.   [48] *Ibid.*, p. 50, n. 1.

risen Christ, when he writes: 'Do you not know that your bodies are limbs and organs of Christ?' The language is indeed violent and the context shows that Paul intended that it should be violent. 'It is of great importance', Robinson remarks, 'to see that when Paul took the term σῶμα and applied it to the Church, what it must have conveyed to him and his readers (to employ a distinction which itself would have surprised him) something *not corporate but corporeal*.'[49] And Robinson continues:

> Consequently, one must be chary of speaking of 'the metaphor' of the Body of Christ. Paul uses the analogy of the human body to elucidate his teaching that Christians form Christ's body. But the analogy holds because they are in literal fact the risen organism of Christ's person in all its concrete reality. What is arresting is his identification of this personality with the Church. But to say that the Church is the body of Christ is no more of a metaphor than to say that the flesh of the incarnate Jesus or the bread of the Eucharist is the body of Christ. None of them is 'like' His body (Paul never says this): each of them *is* the body of Christ, in that each is the physical complement of the one and the same Person and Life. They are all expressions of a single Christology.
>
> It is almost impossible to exaggerate the materialism and crudity of Paul's doctrine of the Church as literally now the resurrection *body* of Christ. The language of 'membership' of a body corporate has become so trite that the idea that the individual can be a 'member' has ceased to be offensive. . . . The body that he has in mind is as concrete and as singular as the body of the Incarnation. His underlying conception is not of a supra-personal collective, but of a specific personal organism. He is not saying anything so weak as that the Church is a society with a common life and governor, but that its unity is that of a single physical entity: disunion is dismemberment. For it is in fact no other than the glorified body of the risen and ascended Christ.[50]

And, in a note, he adds: 'Paul knows no distinction between the ascended body of Christ and His "mystical" body. . . . One could heartily wish that the misleading and unbiblical phrase the "mystical" body had never been invented.'[51]

[49] *The Body*, p. 50.   [50] *Ibid.*, p. 51.
[51] *Ibid.*, p. 52, n. 1.

The metaphor in Rom. 7.4 is one of sexual union; so too is the imagery of I Cor. 6.13–20. The union between Christ and Christian is as exclusive as that of man and wife. Reversion to fornication severs a Christian from the risen body of Christ just as if he had been married to Christ in the flesh. This is all possible only if the Christian has been severed completely by death from his former 'cohabitation' with the *sarx* (cf. Rom. 7.6). The realism of the union of Christ and Christian in the Church is also presented through the image of the 'bride of Christ' (cf. II Cor. 11.2; Eph. 5.22–23). 'In the same way as no clear distinction can be drawn between the flesh-body of Jesus and the body of His resurrection, so there is no real line between the body of His resurrection and the flesh-bodies of those who are risen with Him; for they are members of it.'[52]

With regard to the question of the origin of the doctrine of the Body of Christ, Robinson insists that his own primary concern is with the doctrinal content rather than the external sources of Paul's terminology. However, he specifically rejects the view of A. E. J. Rawlinson[53] that the origin of this doctrine is to be sought in the Eucharist.[54] Robinson, on the contrary, follows E. Mersch, who points to the resurrection-appearance on the road to Damascus as the ultimate explanation (cf. I Cor. 15.1–11; Acts 26.14 f.; 9.4 f.; 22.7 f.). '*The appearance on which Paul's whole faith and apostleship was founded was the revelation of the resurrection body of Christ, not as an individual, but as the Christian Community.*'[55]

Addressing himself to the problem of the one and the many in the Body of Christ, Robinson observes that when our starting-point is the corporative, collective understanding of the *soma Christou*, the most pressing problem is how the many can be one. The multiplicity

[52] *The Body*, p. 53.

[53] 'Corpus Christi' in *Mysterium Christi* (ed. G. K. A. Bell and A. Deissmann), London: Longmans, Green, 1930, pp. 225–244.

[54] 'However significant the Eucharist may have been for Paul's theology of the Body, it is surely clear that it is not a complete explanation. What was it within his own understanding of Christ that made him – and no one else – take this, at first sight, extraordinary leap from the Eucharist to the *Ecclesia* itself as the extension of Christ's human personality?' (*The Body*, p. 57).

[55] *The Body*, p. 58; cf. B. Mersch, *The Whole Christ: The Historical Development of the Doctrine of the Mystical Body in Scripture and Tradition* (tr. J. R. Kelly), London: Dobson, 1939, p. 104.

is obvious but the unity is problematic. The case is just the opposite for Paul whose doctrine of the body is realistic rather than corporative. The singularity of Christ's resurrection body is taken for granted. How it can consist in a multiplicity of persons is the problem. Paul's explanation is that there must be more than one 'member' if there is to be a body at all (cf. I Cor. 12.12), and yet the multiplicity is achieved without prejudice to the unity. For example, in I Cor. 12.12 and 10.17; Rom. 12.5; and Gal. 3.28, the fact of unity stands in the main sentence, whereas the multiplicity is expressed by subordinate clauses or phrases with the sense of 'in spite of'. The various great passages on the Body of Christ stress and demonstrate the inevitable diversity of Christ's operations (cf. I Cor. 12.4–31; Rom. 12.3–8; Eph. 4.1–16). 'But the diversity is one that derives from the pre-existing nature of the unity as organic: it is not a diversity which has to discover or be made into a unity.'[56] It is in the light of this theological perspective that Paul's strictures against certain individualistic practices in connection with the Eucharist should be viewed (cf. I Cor. 11.17–34). The offenders have no sense of the body and therefore are not worthy to eat the Lord's Supper and participate sacramentally in the body of Christ. 'What the communicant receives is Christ in His body, the Church; and the unity of this body is axiomatic.'[57]

In the Old Testament the prevailing principle was that the many are represented by the remnant (cf. Rom. 11) and that is reduced ultimately to the one. Paul sets this principle in reverse. 'Henceforward, it is not the one who represents the many, like the Servant of Jahveh (Isa. 42.1, etc.) or the Son of Man (standing for the whole "people of the saints of the most High", Dan. 7.13-27). Rather, it is the many who represent the one' (cf. Gal. 3.27–29; 3.28; 3.16).[58] The unity that has ensued is inclusive rather than exclusive, and representative rather than vicarious. When it comes to determining *how* Paul conceives this inclusion of the many in the one, one is met with a great variety of expressions. Robinson suggests Gal. 2.20 as

---

[56] *The Body*, p. 60.

[57] *Ibid.*, p. 60, n. 1.

[58] *Ibid.*, p. 61; cf. also O. Cullmann, *Christ and Time: The Primitive Conception of Time and History* (tr. F. Filson), 3rd ed., London: SCM Press, 1962.

the closest of all his expressions of identification with Christ and adopts Mersch's translation: 'I am con-crucified-with Christ.'[59]

Apparently the most satisfying way in which Paul came to express the unity of Christ and the Christian was in the notion of the headship of Christ. The idea was first adumbrated in I Cor. 11.3 and later connected with the theology of the Body only in Colossians and Ephesians where it appears in close association with the doctrine of the *pleroma* of Christ. The most striking expression of this complex of ideas is in Eph. 1.23, which Robinson describes as one of the most disputed verses in the New Testament. The term κεφαλή must be taken in connection with σῶμα, for they are complementary notions (cf. Eph. 1.22; 4.15 f.; 5.23; Col. 1.18; 2.9 f., 19).

> Christ is never spoken of as the head of things in general in a meta-phorical manner, though His universal lordship is of course everywhere presupposed. He is *head* only of His own resurrection body, in which Christians are incorporate. How literally and organically this headship is regarded may be judged from Eph. 4.14–16. . . . The notion of 'growing up into the head', however crude physiologically, is obviously possible only to someone whose thinking through and through is in organic categories.[60]

In the remainder of his book Robinson widens the context of his treatment of the Body of Christ by viewing it in its relation to the whole of salvation-history. The fulness of God which is in Christ must be extended to incorporate every man until all are brought within the One. The circle of Christ's kingship must be filled in and filled out, and the agent of this process is the Church. Its function is to extend throughout Christ's redeemed universe the acknowledgement of his victory.[61] The Church is the covenant people of the new order and the Body has become the sphere of election (Col. 3.15; Eph. 4.4). The Church is most decisively marked off from the old Israel by its possession of the Holy Spirit (Rom. 8.11; I Cor. 12.13;

[59] *The Body*, pp. 62–63.

[60] *Ibid.*, p. 66.

[61] The influence of Oscar Cullmann is particularly noticeable in this section of the book, and in this particular period of his life generally. In addition to *Christ and Time*, cf. also 'The Kingship of Christ and the Church in the New Testament,' in *The Early Church* (ed. A. J. B. Higgins), London: SCM Press, 1956, pp. 105–137.

Eph. 4.4) which stamps it as the eschatological community. This aspect of the Church's nature will be the concern of the next chapter.

In a radio broadcast early in 1963, just prior to the publication of *Honest to God*, Bishop Robinson described himself as a radical in these terms: 'The revolutionary can be an "outsider" to the structure he would see collapse: indeed, he must set himself outside it. But the radical goes to the roots of *his own* tradition. He must love it: he must weep over Jerusalem, even if he has to pronounce its doom. . . . This means that the radical must be a man of roots.'[62] *The Body* is an important book in its own right; it is a significant contribution to the state of the question that we had outlined earlier in the chapter. But it is equally important perhaps for the glimpse it affords of the roots of Bishop Robinson's later un-traditional – indeed, radical – questions that he poses so sharply in *Honest to God* and especially in *The New Reformation?*

The Body is a work of biblical theology and hence is not proposed as a totally adequate and complete ecclesiology. The Pauline doctrine itself is hardly complete. But given the theological area that the book does traverse and, further, despite the lack of any explicit dependence upon any Catholic theologian or exegete apart from two brief references to E. Mersch and a fleeting reference to F. Prat, *The Body: A Study in Pauline Theology* is his most 'Catholic' work, i.e. least open to criticism according to the categories of traditional Catholic theology.[63] One is tempted as well to characterize *The Body* as his best book, but comparisons are hazardous particularly when it is a

[62] Cited in *The Honest to God Debate*, p. 28.

[63] Unlike, for example, his *In the End, God* . . . , wherein he denies the existence of Hell as it is commonly understood in conservative theology (cf. chapter 9, pp. 108–123), even though he takes the subject of Hell with great seriousness (cf. for example, pp. 118–119); *Jesus and His Coming*, wherein he rejects the doctrine of the *Parousia* as a separate event still to be awaited (*passim*; it is at the very heart of his whole argumentation); 'Kingdom, Church and Ministry', in *The Historic Episcopate*, wherein he takes the position that the episcopacy is of the *plene esse* of the Church (cf. pp. 18 ff.); *Honest to God* wherein, among other things, his Christology is open to some question (cf. pp. 64 ff.); and, finally, in his *Christian Morals Today*, wherein, as he himself admits, he stands most firmly in the Protestant tradition.

question of writings of such breadth and diversity as those of John A. T. Robinson. This generally favourable evaluation is not made, however, without some qualification; but first of all a consideration of some of the various reviews of *The Body* would be in order.

The most fundamental criticism levelled against Robinson's analysis of Hebrew anthropology is that of J. Barr in *The Semantics of Biblical Language*.[64] Barr refers to the 'exploitation' of the supposed correspondence of thought structure and linguistic structure in recent theological work and mentions *The Body* as a case in point.[65] He is specifically critical of Robinson's explanation for the fact that the Jews had but one word for the body, i.e. *basar*, while the Greeks had two: *sarx* and *soma*. Robinson had argued that the Greeks, unlike the Jews, required two separate words to express their own philosophical presuppositions.[66] Barr calls this assumption 'self-evidently absurd' and takes him to task for his 'failure to think at all of historical or diachronic semantics, and of such things as the inheritance of a vocabulary stock from the past. . . . It is impossible to understand the distinction of form and matter as having been active in influencing the vocabulary stock at a time hundreds of years before those first philosophers who themselves did not use the distinction.'[67] Barr specifically disavows any attempt to discuss what difference these criticisms would make to the general thesis of Robinson's book, but there is no reason to suggest that the criticisms, if valid, are lethal.[68] Benoit, for example, also expresses reservations about this particular section of Robinson's volume and yet his enthusiasm for the general thesis and argumentation of the book itself is very much apparent.[69] Benoit is of the opinion that Robinson exaggerates the Hebrew attitude toward the body. The Jews, after all, had a spontaneous, commonsense attitude and not an exclusively theological view.[70] The discussion is not an idle one, as Benoit points

[64] London: Oxford University Press, 1961; cf. also *Biblical Words for Time* (Studies in Biblical Theology no. 33), London: SCM Press, 1962.

[65] *Op. cit.*, pp. 34–37; Barr, in fact, questions the whole underlying assumption of G. Kittel's monumental *Wörterbuch* (cf. chapter 8, pp. 206–262).

[66] Cf. *The Body*, pp. 12 ff.   [67] *Semantics*, pp. 36–37.

[68] Barr himself is not easy to evaluate. Cf., for example, R. McL. Wilson's cautious review in *New Testament Studies* 8 (1962) 282–283.

[69] Cf. Benoit's review of *The Body* – *Revue Biblique* 64 (1957) 581.

[70] *Ibid.*, p. 582.

out, because Robinson draws certain inadmissible conclusions from these linguistic presuppositions. For example, the physical and material character of the *soma* would appear to have no particular importance, nor would its role as a principle of individuation.[71] But as Benoit correctly indicates, Robinson's position does not seem to do sufficient justice to Paul's thought (cf. Rom. 8.11, 23; Phil. 3.21; I Cor. 15.49). We are the Body of Christ (I Cor. 12.27) but only insofar as we are his members (I Cor. 12.12–27; Eph. 5.30) and these 'members' are our own bodies (I Cor. 6.15). The notion of individual salvation is also suggested by II Cor. 5.10 (cf. I Cor. 15.42). The orientation of *The Body*, as clearly sketched in the 'Introduction', can readily be endorsed; namely, the emphasis on the growing solidarity towards which mankind must progress. But it seems that this can be developed sufficiently without sacrificing the bodily individuality of those who have been glorified in Christ. 'For it is in Christ and by Christ,' Benoit writes, 'that they receive the newness of life; it is indeed in his Body and by his Body that their bodies share in glory; it is in the Church and by the Church, which is his Body extended to the dimensions of the new Cosmos (the *pleroma* of Colossians and Ephesians), that they are united to Christ and to one another as his members and as members one of another. Thus truly Christ is "all in all" (Col. 3.11). One could not conceive of our solidarity (*collectivism*) in a more satisfying way.'[72]

[71] Cf. *The Body*, p. 32, n. 1: 'Again, creation transfigured at the *Parousia* may or may not be physical – its substance is quite irrelevant.' And yet Robinson does not categorically deny the reality of individual salvation; thus cf. pp. 78–79: 'Our survival (both now and hereafter) as distinct selves depends, for the Bible, not on the body, but upon the fact that everyone is called by God to a unique and eternal relationship with Himself. Paul sees the abiding foundation of individuality in each man's gift from God (1 Cor. 7.7,17) and each man's inalienable responsibility to Him (1 Cor. 3.13–15; 2 Cor. 5.10; Rom. 14.12).' Yet, he adds in a note: 'There is therefore no ultimate distinction between the individual resurrection body and the one resurrection Body. . . .' S. Lyonnet, in contrast to Benoit, does not believe that Robinson has any intention of denying the reality of the risen body in its individuality (cf. *Biblica*, 36 [1955] 108).

[72] *Revue Biblique* 64, p. 584. Other critics have concentrated on Robinson's portrayal of the Pauline usage of *sarx* and *soma*. Cf. W. D. Davies, *Journal of Biblical Literature* 72 (1953) 74–76; C. F. D. Moule, *Journal of Theological Studies* 4 (1953) 74–75; and D. Mollat, 'Bulletin de théologie paulinienne', *Recherches*

The third and final section of *The Body* contains Robinson's specifically ecclesiological development of Pauline theology. It is difficult to disagree with Benoit when he writes: 'If Robinson is not the first to launch this salutary reaction (against the corporative, collective concept of the *soma Christou*), he at least gives it a new force by reason of his vigorous exposition. For my part I can do nothing but applaud him; for it is in this excellent insight and in its consequences that the great interest of the monograph resides.'[73] And Moule's judgement is equally favourable: 'The really great thing about this book is its trenchant presentation of the uncompromising Pauline gospel of the union between Christ and the Church . . . one massive theme has been concentratedly exposed, namely, that Christians are, as such, the Body of Christ.'[74]

There have also been less favourable criticisms of this all-important third chapter; both in general and in specific areas. With regard to Robinson's explanation of the origin of the doctrine, for example, Moule notes that it is simply impossible to prove, even though it is a plausible hypothesis. Cerfaux, on the other hand, insists on a development in Paul's theology as a result of his apostolic labours, and is not inclined to accept the explanation that Robinson borrowed from Mersch.[75]

Benoit offers two criticisms of the section on the problem of the one and the many. First, he disagrees with Robinson in opposing the theme of the Body of Christ (the many represent and constitute the one) and the Servant of Isaiah or the Son of Man of Daniel (the one represents the many). This is unjustifiable because we are *in Christ* in so far as, included in his person as representative of the Servant and the Son of Man, we pass from death to life, from sin to justification, and from corruption to glory; and Christ is *in us* to the extent that he communicates the fruits of salvation and brings to reality in

---

de science religieuse 45 (1957) 240–261. Moule and Mollat are decidedly more favourable in their evaluations than is Davies.

[73] *Art. cit.*, p. 581; cf. also J. Havet's warm praise, *art. cit.* (in *Littérature et Théologie Pauliniennes*), p. 186.

[74] *Art. cit.*, p. 75.

[75] *The Church in the Theology of St Paul*, p. 395.

our individual persons, now collectively regrouped by him, this new humanity which is the Church, his Body, and the centre of the Cosmos which has been recapitulated in Christ as its Head. Benoit's second criticism follows from the first; namely, that Robinson's notions of κεφαλή and πλήρωμα are not exact. Robinson wrote on page 66: 'Christ is never spoken of as the head of things in general in a metaphorical manner, though His universal lordship is of course everywhere presupposed.' Benoit disagrees with this statement and cites Col. 2.10 in refutation. A second statement of Robinson's appearing on the next page (67) is also criticized: '(Pleroma) has no connection with the image of the head and body, and it is a mistake to define it, over against the head, as its "complement", viz., the body.' But these terms can also be understood in a different sense, namely, cosmic. In this sense κεφαλή would be employed with the meaning of supremacy before being combined with the notion of the Body and taking on the meaning of 'Head'.[76]

The remainder of the specific criticisms are directed against material developed in the fifth and final section of the chapter: 'The Old Body and the New'. But since this is concerned more with the Church as the eschatological community, we shall defer our consideration of these observations until the next chapter.

We have thus far mentioned some specific criticisms of the ecclesiological section of The Body, and we have already referred to certain general comments on the study as a whole, for example those of Benoit, Moule, Lyonnet, Havet, and Mollat. The over-all judgement of others, however, has been less enthusiastic. L. P. Pherigo was not persuaded by the arguments of the book, with the exception of Robinson's description of Paul's view of the Church as the Body of Christ. 'Robinson's Paul is too much a Rabbinic Jew, too little influenced by Hellenism, too systematic in his theology, and too closely patterned after the portrait of Paul in Acts.' But the real criticism – and the basic criticism – that has been made against The Body by Protestant reviewers in several cases is this: 'Also, there is a tacit but definite acceptance of Catholic presuppositions. Moreover,

[76] Art. cit. (review of The Body), p. 585; cf. also 'Corps, Tête et Plérôme . . . ', pp. 22–44. The distinction is much clearer in the original French; namely, chef and tête.

this reviewer does not share the author's enthusiasm for Paul's doctrine of the Church as relevant in our times.'[77]

The exact reverse of this observation is our own view. We share Robinson's 'Catholic presuppositions' and his enthusiasm for Paul's doctrine of the Church as relevant in our times. At the beginning of this chapter it was noted that 'with a consideration of the Church as the "Body of Christ", one touches upon the deepest and innermost reality of her nature'.[78] And so to endorse *The Body* as we have done in the course of this chapter is to say something significant about John A. T. Robinson's doctrine of the Church. For in an area of ecclesiology so central as this, he is quite comfortably 'orthodox'. He will appear less so, however, as he proceeds to fill out his ecclesiological perspective in later books and essays that will occupy our attention in subsequent chapters.

[77] *Journal of Bible and Religion* 20 (1952) 275–276; cf. also M. S. Enslin, *Journal of Religion* 33 (1953) 209; H. E. W. Turner, *Church Quarterly Review* 153 (1952) 531–533; and recall also W. D. Davies' remarks on Robinson's inadequate mention of the necessity of faith for baptism (*art. cit.*, p. 76).

[78] P. 21.

3

THE CHURCH:
THE ESCHATOLOGICAL COMMUNITY

HOWEVER central the image of the 'Body of Christ' might be in our ecclesiology, it could never be maintained that this notion is a totally adequate one.[1] As we suggested at the outset of the preceding chapter, the Church is the 'Body of Christ' in a sense determined by the notion of the 'People of God'. In other words, the 'Body of Christ' is a community-in-history, for 'to be "in Christ" is to enter the kingdom present now, which in time to come will embrace the new heavens and the new earth when Christ will again return'.[2] This is tantamount to saying that the 'Body of Christ' is an *eschatological* community.[3]

'It is no accident', John A. T. Robinson has written, 'that the failure to relate the Church properly to the Kingdom should issue also in the failure to relate the Ministry properly to the Church.

[1] This is certainly the position adopted by Pope Paul VI in his opening address to the second session of the Second Vatican Council: *AAS* 55 (1963) 848; translation in *Council Speeches of Vatican II* (ed. H. Küng, Y. Congar, and D. O'Hanlon), Glen Rock, New Jersey: Paulist Press, 1964, pp. 25–26.

[2] G. E. Wright, *God Who Acts: Biblical Theology as Recital* (Studies in Biblical Theology, no. 8), London: SCM Press, 1952, p. 64. The significance of this fact has not always been recognized by classical Protestant theology, as O. Cullmann has suggested; cf. *Christ and Time: The Primitive Christian Conception of Time and History* (3rd ed.), pp. 146–147, and *The Christology of the New Testament* (tr. S. Guthrie and C. Hall), Philadelphia: Westminster, 1959, pp. 233–234, cf. also p. 193.

[3] The need for a fuller development of this concept of the Church as the eschatological community has been stressed recently by R. Schnackenburg, *New Testament Theology Today* (tr. D. Askew), New York: Herder, 1963, p. 120, and Y. Congar in his Foreword to F. B. Norris's *God's Own People*, Baltimore: Helicon, 1962, p. v.

Both reflect a more fundamental failure to retain the eschatological perspective of the New Testament. . . . We shall not get our theology of the Church and the Ministry right until we get our eschatology right.'[4] 'As long as the Church is working with inadequate eschatological categories,' he has written elsewhere, 'its life will be stifled precisely at the points where it shows most signs of renewal. . . . There can be no theme upon which the Church owes it to itself and to its Lord to work out its preaching more urgently and more thoroughly than its gospel of eschatology.'[5]

We are concerned here with two distinct but interrelated questions; namely, the nature and content of New Testament eschatology and, secondly, the application of this perspective to the Church. We have already seen what it means to be a community in Christ. It will be the task of this chapter to consider this community in its historical context, specifically in its relationship to the Kingdom of God. And as was the case in the previous chapter, we are confronted with questions of exegesis and of theology. Robinson has sought through his various writings to unite the conclusions and perspectives of each. The question must be asked whether, in the process of fusion, he has preserved a proper ecclesiological balance.

Our method will be similar to that of the previous chapter. First, there will be a very brief consideration of the current state of the question, both exegetical and theological, including pertinent references to the dogmatic constitution *De Ecclesia*, of the Second Vatican Council. Secondly, there will be presented an exposition of Robinson's position with regard to (*a*) various exegetical questions surrounding New Testament eschatology and (*b*) the relationship of this biblical data to ecclesiology. Finally, there will be offered a critique of Robinson's views, taking into account the review-evaluations of various New Testament exegetes and theologians. The emphasis, however, will always remain on the theological rather than the strictly exegetical questions. In this chapter we are considering New Testatment eschatology and related exegetical problems only in so far as they might illuminate and clarify the central

---

[4] 'Kingdom, Church and Ministry', in *The Historic Episcopate*, chapter I, pp. 11–22, cf. p. 17.

[5] *In the End, God* . . . , p. 128.

ecclesiological question at hand; namely, in what sense can it be proposed that the Church, the Body of Christ, is the eschatological community? And, further, in what sense does John A. T. Robinson understand this designation?

The issues to be treated in this chapter are very important for a proper understanding of Robinson's theology of the Church, more so even than the previous chapter on the Church as the Body of Christ. From his concept of the Church as the eschatological community and, more specifically, from his view of the fundamental relationship between Church and Kingdom, will develop his notions of ministry, liturgy, and the whole mission of the Church.

STATE OF THE QUESTION

1. *The Eschatology of the New Testament*[6]

The term 'eschatology' embraces a number of different concepts and has been applied in various instances to the end of individuals and of the world. But even the principal terms 'end' and 'world' have been understood in several ways.[7] For the sake of clarity and consistency, we shall accept B. Rigaux's definition of 'eschatology': 'the ensemble of teaching and expressions concerning the expected intervention of God in time, in virtue of which the present state of

[6] For the general outline of the history of the exegesis we have relied especially upon B. Rigaux, 'La Seconde Venue de Jésus,' in *La Venue du Messie: Messianisme et Eschatologie* (E. Massaux *et al.*), Louvain: Desclée de Brouwer, 1962, pp. 173–216, cf. especially pp. 173–177; W. G. Kümmel, 'Futurische und präsentische Eschatologie im ältesten Urchristentum,' *New Testament Studies* 5 (1958–9) 113–126, especially pp. 113–118; and F. M. Braun, *Aspects nouveaux du problème de l'Eglise*, Fribourg: Librairie de l'Université, 1941, who, in turn, has made use of F. Holmström, *Das eschatologische Denken der Gegenwart*, Gütersloh, 1936.

[7] John A. T. Robinson expresses his own view in his earliest book, *In the End, God . . .* , p. 54; 'What the investigation of *kairos* and *chronos* has shown is that there is not necessarily a simple correspondence between temporal and moral finality. *To claim that there is is always to exalt temporal quality above the moral as the determining factor.* It is to reverse the eschatological equation: to say that the final in time is the ultimate in significance, rather than that the ultimate in significance is the final in time. Now for such reversal there are no valid grounds. The last in a temporal series, *just because it is the last*, has no more importance than any other event: it can claim no ultimacy for the purposes of interpretation'.

reality will cease and will be replaced by an economy that will entail an entirely new relationship between God and his creation'.[8]

While this might be agreed upon readily as a working definition, there exists a very serious controversy regarding the New Testament's eschatological perspective. At one extreme there are the 'consequent eschatologists' who insist that for Jesus the Kingdom of God was a purely future reality which would not be realized until soon after his own death,[9] and at the other extreme there are the 'realized eschatologists' who insist that the Kingdom is essentially a present reality.[10] There are several variants in between.[11]

2. Eschatology and Ecclesiology: The Relation of Church and Kingdom

F. M. Braun, in his oft-quoted survey, *Aspects nouveaux du problème*

[8] *Art. cit.*, p. 173: ' . . . l'ensemble des enseignements et des représentations touchant l'intervention attendue de Dieu dans le temps, en vertu de laquelle l'état actuel des choses cessera et fera place à une économie entièrement nouvelle entre Dieu et sa création.'

[9] Cf., for example, A. Schweitzer, *Geschichte der Leben-Jesu-Forschung* (6th ed.) Tübingen, 1951; J. Weiss, *Die Predigt Jesu vom Reiche Gottes* (2nd ed.), Göttingen, 1900; M. Werner, *Die Entstehung des christlichen Dogmas* (2nd ed.), Berne, 1953; and E. Grässer, *Das Problem der Parusieverzögerung in den synoptischen Evangelien und in der Apostelgeschichte*, Berlin: Töpelmann, 1957.

[10] Cf., for example, C. H. Dodd, *The Parables of the Kingdom* (rev. ed.), London: Collins, 1961, and *The Apostolic Preaching and its Developments*, New York: Harpers & Brothers, 1962 (orig. ed. 1936); T. F. Glasson, *The Second Advent: The Origin of the New Testament Doctrine* (3rd rev. ed.), London: Epworth Press, 1963 (orig. ed. 1945).

[11] Cf., for example, W. G. Kümmel, *Promise and Fulfilment: The Eschatological Message of Jesus* (Studies in Biblical Theology, no. 23; tr. D. M. Barton), London: SCM Press, 1961; Kümmel's position is endorsed by E. Schweizer, *Church Order in the New Testament* (Studies in Biblical Theology, no. 32; tr. F. Clarke), London: SCM Press, 1961, p. 20 [2,a.]; cf. also O. Cullmann, *Christ and Time*; 'Eschatology and Missions in the New Testament,' (tr. O. Wyon), in *The Background of the New Testament and its Eschatology: Essays in Honour of C. H. Dodd* (ed. W. D. Davies and D. Daube), Cambridge: University Press, 1956, pp. 409–421; and 'L'Evangile johannique et l'histoire du salut,' *New Testament Studies* 11 (1965) 111–122; R. Bultmann, 'History and Eschatology in the New Testament,' *New Testament Studies* 1 (1954–55) 5–16, and *The Presence of Eternity: History and Eschatology*, New York: Harper & Brothers, 1957; R. H. Fuller, *The Mission and Achievement of Jesus* (Studies in Biblical Theology, no. 12), London: SCM Press, 1954; R. Schnackenburg, *God's Rule and Kingdom* (tr. J. Murray), London: Nelson, 1963; A. Feuillet, 'Parousie,' *Dictionnaire de la Bible, Supplément*, fasc. 35, Paris,

de l'Église,[12] has called attention to the new ecclesiological consensus that has developed among Protestants, following upon a gradual but decisive shift away from the assumptions and presuppositions of Liberalism. The Church is seen as the People of God, which has been called together by him, and not simply as a community or federation of communities issuing from the free will of men. The Church is indeed a messianic community and therefore an eschatological community, because it looks toward and works for the realization of the total rule of God over creation and all mankind. The mission of the Church flows from her nature; namely, she exists to orient the present world toward the future Kingdom where God will be all in all. The Church, then, is the instrument of the Kingdom, *but it is not itself the Kingdom.* For Braun this position is perhaps the most significant characteristic of recent Protestant ecclesiology: the refusal to identify Church and Kingdom.[13] A typical expression of this view is given by K. L. Schmidt:

> The eschatological presuppositions of Jesus' self-designation as Son of Man, and of the institution of the Lord's Supper, prove that the idea of the Church also is eschatological. But this does not mean that Church and Kingdom of God are the same thing. They are not the same in the early Church, which certainly regarded itself as the ἐκκλησία while continuing the proclamation of the Kingdom. Nor are they the same in the preaching of Jesus, for he promised the Kingdom of God to his Church, i.e. the Church which he founded. The ἐκκλησία after Easter regarded itself as eschatological in this sense. Similarly the individual Christian may be called eschatological, because he is a justified sinner.[14]

While a consensus regarding the non-identity of Church and Kingdom may have indeed been reached among Protestant authors, such unanimity certainly does not exist when the question is pressed

---

1960, col. 1331–1419, and 'La triomphe du Fils de l'Homme d'après la déclaration du Christ aux Sanhédrites (Mc. xiv, 62; Mt. xxvi, 64; Lc. xxii, 69),' in *La venue du Messie*, pp. 149–171; and B. Rigaux, *art. cit.*

[12] *Op. cit.*, cf. p. 46, n. 6 above.

[13] *Aspects nouveaux*, pp. 103 ff., 161–170.

[14] 'The Church' (tr. J. Coates) in *Bible Key Words* from G. Kittel's *Theologische Wörterbuch zum Neuen Testament*, vol. 1, New York: Harper and Brothers, 1951, pp. 41–42.

further and greater precision is sought. What *is* the relationship between Church and Kingdom? What is the *nature* of this eschatological community?

At the risk of over-simplifying we would suggest, following H. G. Hamilton,[15] that there are three principal approaches to these questions: the existentialist interpretation of Bultmann, the 'realized' or 'inaugurated eschatology' of Dodd and Robinson, and the salvation-history perspective of Cullmann.

It is Cullmann rather than Dodd who has exerted the greater influence in this particular area of Robinson's ecclesiology.[16] Cullmann's position is adequately presented and developed in his essay, 'The Kingship of Christ and the Church in the New Testament'.[17] Fundamental to Cullmann's argument is not only the distinction between the Church and the Kingdom of God, but also between the Kingdom of God and the Kingdom of Christ. The Kingdom of Christ and the Church are also distinct, but they coincide chronologically at least, whereas the Kingdom of God is a purely future quantity. The Christian has grounds for expecting the Kingdom of God because he knows that the Kingdom of Christ has already begun through the death and resurrection of Christ. The effective beginning was at the Ascension and the end of the Kingdom of Christ will come after the Second Coming, which itself is the final act of the Kingdom of Christ. The Kingdom of Christ, therefore, belongs to the eschatological future and is 'a kind of recapitulation of the phase which is to follow it'.[18]

The eschatological problem of the New Testament is contained in this tension between the present and the future. A proper understanding of the notion of the Kingdom of Christ is important because 'the time of the Church can be defined in just the same

---

[15] 'The Last Things in the Last Decade: The Significance of Recent Study in the Field of Eschatology', *Interpretation* 14 (1960) 131–142.

[16] This is especially evident in *The Body* and in 'Kingdom, Church and Ministry'.

[17] The essay appears in *The Early Church* (ed. A. J. B. Higgins), London: SCM Press, 1956, pp. 105–137. Cullmann's views are elsewhere expressed in *Christ and Time*, and *The Christology of the New Testament*, especially chapter 7, 'Jesus the Lord', pp. 195–237.

[18] *The Early Church*, p. 113.

way'.[19] The Spirit is the element of the future Kingdom of God, and so at Pentecost the Church finds herself at the opening stage of the realization of the people of God in the end of time. The same tension that exists in the Kingdom of Christ also exists in the Church. The Spirit is already present in the Church, but only as a 'pledge' of what is to come (II Cor. 1.22) and as the 'first-fruits' of the future harvest (Rom. 8.23). Yet, despite the fact that the Church and the Kingdom of Christ exhibit the same tension and coincide in time, there are also important differences between the two realities.

In Colossians and Ephesians Christ is described as 'head' of all creation (Col. 2.10; Eph. 1.10) and as 'head' of the Church (Col. 1.18; Eph. 1.22).[20] This does not mean, however, that the Church is a mere section of the Kingdom of Christ. While the place of the Church is narrower, i.e. it does not equal *all* creation, it is nonetheless not subordinate. 'This concentration on one definite point of creation, the earthly world and, within this world, a human community, signifies rather that the Church is the heart and centre of the *Regnum Christi*. It is not merely a section but the only point from which the whole of the *Regnum Christi* can be seen, and whatever happens in the Church has a decisive influence throughout the *Regnum Christi*, just as the unique work of the earthly, incarnate Christ was decisive for the subjection of the whole creation.'[21] The Church, then, is part of the whole sphere of the *Regnum Christi* of which Christ is the head, and yet Christ himself is present in this limited part of his kingdom in a way that is very different from his presence elsewhere. 'The Church of Christ', Cullmann concludes, 'forms the narrowly confined early setting of the *Regnum Christi* which Christ, the head of the whole creation, has chosen for his earthly body.'[22]

The Kingdom of Christ and the Church are always to be distinguished by reason of membership. 'The fact that the members of the Church are conscious of all this, that they know that Christ rules,

[19] *The Early Church*, p. 116.

[20] Robinson, of course, would insist that, strictly speaking, 'head' is the corollary of 'body'. In Colossians and Ephesians Christ is *not* described as *head* of all creation as well as head of the Church. (Cf. *The Body*, p. 66.)

[21] *The Early Church*, p. 123.   [22] *Ibid.*, p. 126.

and are therefore members of the Kingdom of Christ consciously, is what distinguishes them as a Church from all the other members of the *Regnum Christi* who may be its servants unconsciously.'[23] The Church must be viewed in the context of salvation-history. The Church is a 'remnant' as Israel was the *qehal Yahweh*, the ἐκκλησία. The concept of 'vicariousness' provides the key to an understanding of the whole biblical concept of the scheme of salvation. Throughout the Old Testament the process is one of progressive reduction: from Israel to the tiny remnant and finally to the person of Christ, the Servant of Yahweh and the Son of Man. In the New Testament and during the time of the Church the process is reversed, but the principle of 'vicariousness' remains in force. The Church is the Body of Christ, i.e. she is the principle of representation in the process of development from the One to the many. She is 'the earthly centre from which the full Lordship of Christ becomes visible'.[24] This, in fact, is the essential mark of the Church, that she acknowledges the Lordship of Christ. Therefore, her first task is the preaching of the Gospel. 'The coming of the Kingdom of God does not depend on whether the Church is great or small on the day which God has appointed for the end of the age. But the Church must do that to which it is called, preach the Gospel to all.'[25] In this central task the Church cannot be discouraged by failure, since the greatest earthly failure that ever was is at the very centre of the faith of the New Testament: the cross of Christ, which means victory for the Christian over all hostile powers and the eschatological beginning of the present Kingdom of Christ which can only be superseded by the Kingdom of God.[26]

No consensus exists among Catholic theologians and exegetes regarding the identity or non-identity of Church and Kingdom of God.[27] The most satisfying discussion is presented by R. Schnackenburg in his *God's Rule and Kingdom*. Schnackenburg writes:

---

[23] *The Early Church*, p. 128.   [24] *Christ and Time*, p. 156.

[25] *The Early Church*, p. 133.

[26] For a critique of Cullmann's thesis, cf. R. Schnackenburg, *God's Rule and Kingdom*, pp. 296 ff., 343 ff.

[27] Some theologians, such as C. Journet, prefer to emphasize the basis for identity between the Church and the Kingdom; cf. his *L'Eglise du Verbe Incarné*, vol. II, Paris: Desclée de Brouwer (2nd ed.), 1962, p. 997, n. 1. Others, particu-

God's reign is not so associated with the Church that we can speak of it as a 'present form of God's kingdom', since this would suppose an amalgamation with the Church's history on earth. God's reign as such has no organization and goes through no process; it does not embrace the just and sinners, it is in no sense dependent upon earthly and human factors. It is not 'built up' by men and thus brought to its goal. Yet all this can be said of the Church in its mundane form. . . .

The relation of Church to *basileia* is clearly and beautifully brought out in the *Didache*: 'Be mindful, O Lord, of the Church, rescue her from all evil and perfect her in thy love, and bring her together from the four winds, her whom thou hast made holy, into thy kingdom which thou hast prepared for her' (10.5).[28]

A further distinction must be made between the eschatological community which is the Church and the perfect eschatological society. This distinction is made on the basis of membership. The Judgement will bring into the redeemed community of the perfect *basileia* other men who did not know Jesus in their lifetime (Matt. 25.34–40) and who evidently were not members of his visible eschatological community, the Church. And, on the other hand, certain unfaithful and unworthy members of the earthly community will be rejected and cast out (Matt. 7.22 ff.; Luke 13.16 ff.; Matt. 13.24–30, 36–43, 47–50; and 22.11–13). Schnackenburg draws certain consequences from this particular relationship between Church and Kingdom: (1) While the two are not identical, they are related by reason of the fact that the community established by and attached to Jesus has a share in the saving graces of the present and the promises for the future. (2) The main significance of the community consists in its orientation towards the future kingdom; it is the community of those who look for the Kingdom of God. (3) The forces of God's present reign are active in Jesus' community as in Jesus himself on account of the powers Jesus communicated to his disciples and especially to Peter, i.e. the authority to teach and forgive, the Word and the Spirit. (4) The Church is an *ecclesia*

---

larly exegetes, have adopted more moderate positions; cf., for example, A. Feuillet, 'Le règne de Dieu et la personne de Jésus d'après les Evangiles synoptiques', *Introduction à la Bible*, vol. 2 (ed. A. Robert and A. Feuillet), Tournai: Desclée, 1959, pp. 801 ff.

[28] *God's Rule and Kingdom*, pp. 233–234.

militans et pressa, an *ecclesia crucis*, i.e. it must do constant battle against the powers of evil and must suffer affliction and persecution. (5) Membership in this eschatological community does not in itself guarantee acceptance into the future Kingdom, but presupposes loyalty even to the point of martyrdom. (6) The basic thought, uniting present and future, must be that of the eschatological people of God, as assembled and also as scattered throughout the world.[29]

As we shall see in our exposition of Robinson's doctrine of the Church as the eschatological community later in this chapter, the bishop lays heavy stress upon the distinction between Church and Kingdom and is particularly concerned that our doctrine of the Kingdom should always be higher than our doctrine of the Church.[30] Enough has been said already in our survey of the state of the question to rule out of court any assertion that Robinson, by reason of his stand *vis-à-vis* the Church–Kingdom relationship, veers necessarily from Catholic orthodoxy. The assumptions of Braun and Journet, to cite but two examples, are no longer accepted without criticism, as the recent work of R. Schnackenburg especially demonstrates.

3. *The Church as the Eschatological Community according to the Second Vatican Council*

The dogmatic constitution of the Second Vatican Council, *De Ecclesia*, serves to complement rather than displace earlier magisterial texts such as the encyclical, *Mystici Corporis*. The notion of the Church as the eschatological community is given some measure of prominence in this decree whereas the eschatological perspective was practically absent from the aforementioned encyclical. It is not of the nature of a dogmatic constitution, ordinarily, to solve exegetical questions or put an end to theological discussion, and, given the aims and orientation of the Second Vatican Council as a pastoral rather

[29] *God's Rule and Kingdom*, cf. pp. 230–232.
[30] Thus, he writes in his essay, 'Kingdom, Church and Ministry', p. 17: 'Just as the NT bids us have as high a doctrine of the ministry as we like, as long as our doctrine of the Church is higher, so it commands us have as high a doctrine of the Church as we may, provided our doctrine of the Kingdom is higher. And this conclusion is of no mere academic consequence. It must govern all our assessments as Christians, including those about Church union.'

than a doctrinally-minded assembly, we should not expect to discover ready-made answers to the various questions thus far posed. Nevertheless, a brief summary of the constitution would be in order both to fill out and bring up to date the state of the question, as we have outlined it in the preceding pages.

The nature of the Church as the eschatological community is set in bold relief when viewed in the light of salvation-history. She was foreshadowed in the history of the people of Israel, constituted and made manifest by the outpouring of the Spirit, and now looks toward the glorious consummation at the end of time.[31] This glorious consummation consists in the perfection of the Kingdom of God, already inaugurated by God upon the earth to be further extended until it is brought to this point of perfection by him when 'creation itself will be delivered from its slavery to corruption into the freedom of the glory of the sons of God' (Rom. 8.21). And yet the present state of the Church does not seem to correspond to the grandeur and glory that awaits it at the end, when all things will be re-established in Christ (Eph. 1.4–5, 10). This messianic people does not actually include all men, or even the majority of men. It is indeed a small Church in a large world, to borrow Congar's description.[32] Nevertheless, this same community is a lasting and certain seed of unity, hope and salvation for the whole human race. 'Established by Christ as a communion of life, charity and truth, it is also used by Him as an instrument for the redemption of all, and is sent forth into the whole world as the light of the world and the salt of the earth (cf. Matt. 5.13–16).'[33] She is the new Israel which, while living in the present age, goes in search of a future and abiding city (cf. Heb. 13.14). She is indeed the pilgrim Church (*Ecclesia peregrinans*) pertaining and committed to this age but always looking toward the renovation of the final age and the full realization of the Kingdom of God.[34]

The Church as the eschatological community, therefore, is characterized by a tension between the present and the future, between inauguration and completion, between promise and fulfilment. The Church is 'the Kingdom of Christ now present in

---

[31] Chapter I, para. 2.
[32] *The Wide World My Parish* (tr. D. Attwater), Baltimore: Helicon, 1961, p. 8.
[33] Chapter II, para. 9.   [34] Chapter VII, para. 48.

mystery, (growing) visibly through the power of God in the world'.[35]
But before all else, 'the kingdom is clearly visible in the very person
of Christ, the Son of God and the Son of Man, who came "to serve
and to give His life as a ransom for many" (Mark 10.45).' Jesus is
the source of the Church's gifts and of her mission 'to proclaim and to
spread among all peoples the kingdom of Christ and of God and to
be, on earth, the initial budding-forth of that kingdom'.[36] While it
slowly grows, the Church strains toward the completed kingdom,
with the hope and desire of ultimate union in glory with her King.
And the 'pledge' (Eph. 1.14) and 'first fruits' (Rom. 8.23) of this
glorious destiny is always the Spirit.

The Church is the eschatological community because it is a
community-in-history and a community-in-the-Spirit. Without this
twofold dimension there can be no ecclesiology which is faithful
to the New Testament and to the Gospel. It will be in this light and
with this norm that we shall examine the ecclesiological thought of
Bishop John A. T. Robinson.

THE CHURCH AS THE ESCHATOLOGICAL COMMUNITY
ACCORDING TO BISHOP ROBINSON

1. *The Eschatology of the New Testament*

Robinson's position with regard to New Testament eschatology
is amply developed in his exegetical study, *Jesus and His Coming:
The Emergence of a Doctrine*, published in 1957. It is a book which
occupies a regularly prominent place in the current discussion.
While it contains very little reference to the Church as the eschatological community (he is more concerned here with the role of the
Church in changing the original teaching of Jesus), the work
deserves our study and attention because it offers us some further
insight into the presuppositions of Bishop Robinson's ecclesiology.
In the final part of this chapter we will examine these presuppositions
in a wider context. For the moment it will be sufficient to summarize
the views of John A. T. Robinson, as exegete, as a prelude to our

---

[35] Chapter I, para. 3.   [36] Chapter I, para. 5.

subsequent analysis of his position as theologian, and more specifically as ecclesiologist.

The principal object of interest in the study is the doctrine of the
Second Coming of Christ. The fact of the Church's expectation of
Jesus is not open to dispute, so central is it to the New Testament
hope. The simplest explanation of this fact is that Jesus himself was
the source of this expectation, that he himself led the Church to look
for the *Parousia* – the coming of Christ from heaven to earth in
manifest and final glory. But Robinson raises the question: does the
evidence of the New Testament support this seemingly obvious
explanation as the true one?

First Thessalonians establishes the fact that Paul had taught the
Parousia prior to AD 50; consequently, Robinson begins with a study
of the *logia* of Jesus in the Gospel as the possible source of Paul's
teaching. He divides the *logia* into two classes consisting of the theme
of vindication (victory coming out of defeat) on the one hand, and
the theme of visitation (a coming among men in power and judgement) on the other. The vindication sayings (Matt. 11.12; Mark
8.31–38; 10.35–40; 14.62; Luke 12.50; 13.32; 22.15–18) are not
assertions of a return *from* God, but of a return *to* God. And certain
of the visitation sayings pertain only to the historical ministry of
Jesus, e.g. the parable of the vinedressers, Mark 12.1–12. However,
there is a second class of visitation sayings which would appear to
have undergone a development from their original application by
Jesus to his historical ministry in favour of the idea of his *Parousia*.
Following Dodd and Jeremias, Robinson notes that the evangelists
applied certain of the parables to the post-resurrection Church,
whereas originally they were a warning by Jesus to his contempor-
aries of the crisis facing them. This would apply to the parables of
the talents (Matt. 25.14–30), the gold pieces (Luke 19.12–27), the
watchful porter (Mark 13.33–37), the householder (Luke 12.35–38),
the thief (Luke 12.39 f.), the faithful servant (Matt. 24.45–51), and
the ten virgins (Matt. 25.1–13). 'The parables were spoken',
Robinson writes, 'not to a future situation which had not even
begun – to alert the Church for its Lord's return – but to the present
crisis of the nation, when after so long a period of delegated responsibility its leaders were being faced with the use they had made

of the privileges and opportunities God had accorded to them.'[37] Every reference of Jesus to the 'coming of the Son of Man' refers to his ministry alone, with its climax and its consequences:

> The visitation in judgement of which he spoke would indeed merely be *set in motion* by his rejection. Its outworking, like his own vindication, would take place 'from now on'. As in glory, so in visitation, we must speak not of a realized, but of an inaugurated eschatology, of the Son of Man 'coming to his own' in all the power of God, till the kingdoms of this world shall have become the kingdom of God and of his Christ. For Jesus the messianic act would certainly not be exhausted in his death and resurrection. On the contrary, this moment would but release and initiate that reign of God in which *henceforth* the Father's redeeming work could be brought to the fulfilment which hitherto it was denied.
> But what fails is the evidence that Jesus thought of the messianic act as taking place in two stages, the first of which was now shortly to be accomplished, the second of which would follow after an interval and must in the meantime be the focus of every eye and thought.[38]

The Church's *Parousia* hope does not go back to Jesus. How then are we to bridge the gap between the teaching of Jesus (*c.* AD 30) and the expectation of the Church as described by Paul in I Thessalonians? And 'nothing is more certain than that the transition was made'.[39] Jesus had stood in the prophetic rather than the apocalyptic tradition. The Church translated the eschatology of Jesus into the thought-forms of apocalyptic. The process can be traced throughout the development of the Synoptic tradition, reaching its climax in the Gospel of Matthew. The transition, of course, does not admit of conclusive proof, but it is certainly plausible in that it follows the same pattern as the Old Testament transition from the eschatology of the prophets to that of the apocalyptic writers. 'As in Judaism earlier, the indissoluble unity between the ethical and the eschatological is severed. The "ethics" of Jesus come to be separated out, detached from their eschatological setting, and adapted to the ordered life of the Church. In the same way, the eschatological

---

[37] *Jesus and His Coming*, p. 66; cf. also C. H. Dodd, *Parables of the Kingdom*, pp. 146–153 and J. Jeremias, *The Parables of Jesus* (tr. S. H. Hooke), revised ed., London: SCM Press, 1963, pp. 59–62.

[38] *Jesus and His Coming*, p. 81.   [39] *Ibid.*, p. 83.

elements are assembled and schematized to provide a map for the future and a programme for its hope.'[40]

By way of what might be described aptly as an extended parenthetical remark, Robinson is careful to point out that, in drawing attention to this process of separation and in questioning the primitive character of the apocalyptic strain in the message of Jesus, he does not mean to suggest that Jesus himself taught a purely 'realized eschatology' and that the futurist elements in the Gospel tradition are simply the creation of the Church. Calling attention to certain ambiguities in the notion of 'realized eschatology', Robinson once again argues on behalf of the expression, 'inaugurated eschatology'. All is inaugurated, yet *only* inaugurated. With the coming of the Passion, the great 'henceforth' could at last be pronounced. But the Church later proclaimed that all was *not* inaugurated, that some elements still lay purely in the future.[41]

In support of his hypothesis Robinson analyses the *Parousia* passages of I and II Thessalonians which reveal two types of description of the *Parousia*: the apocalyptic and the non-apocalyptic. The apocalyptic terminology (the coming of the Lord, the trumpet of God, our gathering together with him, the angels of his power, etc.) has affinity with the editorial insertions in the eschatological discourse of Matthew. The non-apocalyptic terminology bears resemblance to the discourses in Luke 21 and Mark 13, both of which are, presumably, closer to the primitive tradition of the Synoptics. Consequently, he concludes that the New Testament idea of the return of Jesus has its origin in the development of apocalyptic in the primitive Church. He summarizes his argument in this way: '. . . of the eschatological material in Thessalonians, the more apocalyptic the passage, the remoter its connexion with anything in the Gospel tradition which may claim to be primitive or provide evidence for the teaching of Jesus. . . . On the other hand, the less apocalyptic the eschatological material in Thessalonians, the closer appears to be its connexion with the Gospel

---

[40] *Jesus and His Coming*, p. 98; cf. pp. 99–100 for his criticism of the Liberal school, i.e. Harnack and Schweitzer.

[41] Cf., pp. 100–102; cf. also *In the End, God* .`. . , pp. 54, 57, 66; 'Resurrection in the NT,' in *The Interpreter's Dictionary of the Bible*, p. 51; and 'Theologians of Our Time: C. H. Dodd,' *Expository Times* 75 (1964) 100–102.

tradition, and with those strata of it which, on the basis of Synoptic criticism, may be regarded as most primitive.'[42]

The emergence of the *Parousia* doctrine in the Church followed three discernible stages: the period of Jesus' preaching, which stressed his ministry as the time of visitation; the period immediately after the death of Jesus when the Christians would have applied his warnings to the worsening political situation in Palestine (Mark 13.1–23, omitting 24–27, the apocalyptic passage); and the period in which apocalyptic development applied his teaching to the End.

> But though the influence of the *Parousia* idea cannot be demonstrated with certainty till a relatively late stage in the tradition, this may always be said to be due to the scantiness of our evidence. And indeed the argument from silence would again be precarious, were it not for the complementary fact that in each of the cases we have examined – the original teaching of Jesus; the first apostolic preaching; the primitive creeds; and the earliest state of the Gospel tradition – there are always the marks of a single, self-consistent alternative, from which mention of a subsequent *Parousia* shows no sign of having been accidentally or fortuitously omitted. This alternative consists in a fully integrated eschatology, according to which, from the Resurrection onwards, the Christ comes in power to his own, till all is finally subjected to that saving sovereignty which God has willed to accomplish through him.[43]

But if this was really the earliest theology of both Jesus and the Church, why was it broken up? Why was the eschatological event divided into two separate acts? Why did Christ come to be expected twice? Robinson insists that his solution can be regarded as no more than a hypothesis, until some better hypothesis is forthcoming. He suggests that the explanation is to be sought in the unresolved crisis in the Christology of the primitive Church with regard to the consummation of the messianic event. Had it taken place already or not? Has *the Christ* come or not? 'The solution, as so often, was a compromise: part of it had taken place and part of it had not, the Christ had come and yet would come. Hence the idea of the messianic drama in two acts separated by an interval.'[44]

[42] *Jesus and His Coming*, p. 105; for the argument presented in some detail, cf. pp. 106–117.

[43] *Ibid.*, pp. 138–139.   [44] *Ibid.*, p. 142.

The turning of the Church to wait for a second coming, appears to arise directly from the hesitation whether *this* piece of history *could*, fully, be called the messianic or eschatological event – not, of course, the End, in the sense of the last thing to happen, but the event that introduces into the world that by which God's purpose for it is finally declared and by which ultimately it must be saved and judged. . . . And that hesitation was never overcome. What of those aspects of the promised messianic rule which seemed to find no fulfilment in Jesus under the form of a servant? As in the Old Testament, unfulfilled prophecy was to prove the father of apocalyptic: features in the traditional picture of God's coming to reign, combined with those in Jesus' own teaching which did not yet appear to have been accounted for, materialized into a second, mythological event still to be awaited.[45]

Robinson attempts to demonstrate this hypothesis through an equally hypothetical exegesis of Acts 3.20–21 wherein there is reflected an original uncertainty whether Jesus was to be considered the Christ *to be* or whether he was *already* the Christ. Acts 2 presents a theology of the Christ 'presently active in his Church through the power of the Spirit'; whereas Acts 3.20–21 depicts him as 'the absentee Christ, inoperative in heaven . . . because he has not yet been sent'.[46] Since there is no further development of this doctrine of Acts 3, Robinson believes that the tension between Jesus as the Christ *to be* and the Christ *in fact* was resolved by the rejection of Acts 3 and the declaration that Jesus is *both* the Christ who has come and the Christ who shall come.

In order to recover 'the wholeness of the Christian hope [and] to find again the unity of the Christ who has come and of the Christ who shall come in the Christ who comes',[47] Robinson turns finally to the Gospel of John, where he finds support for his idea of an 'inaugurated eschatology'. The perfect is the characteristic tense of the Gospel, implying both a present and a future: 'the hour is coming and now is' (4.23; 5.25; cf. 16.32). 'This is the rubric by which the whole theology of John must be interpreted, and by which he holds together, as no other Evangelist does, the period of the Incarnation

[45] *Jesus and His Coming*, p. 151.
[46] *Ibid.*, p. 153; cf. also 'The Most Primitive Christology of All?', *Twelve New Testament Studies*, pp. 139–153.
[47] *Jesus and His Coming*, p. 159.

and the period of the Church.'[48] All the classic apocalyptic themes
are present in John's Gospel – the injunction against alarm, the
forewarning against apostasy, the prediction of travail and tribula-
tion and of persecution for the sake of his name, the need for witness,
the promise of the Spirit as the disciples' advocate, the reference to
the last day – yet with John all these are linked 'not with a second
supernatural event but with the single historical crisis of the death
and resurrection of Jesus. This is the *telos*, the End; and its tense is no
longer the future (Matt. 24.14; Mark 13.7) but the perfect (John
19.28, 30).'[49] For John the *Parousia* is not a separate catastrophic
occurrence, but a continuous pervasion of the daily life of the
disciple and the Church. 'The coming is an abiding presence. . . .
It is the Passion which makes possible and inaugurates the *Parousia
from now on*. The going of Christ to the Father itself initiates the
coming of Christ from the Father.'[50] *Parousia* and Resurrection are
one and the same event, the latter inaugurating the former. 'On the
Cross Jesus goes to the Father, he lives; at the Resurrection and
onwards the disciples live in him and he in them. It is this mutual
indwelling in love, which is the essence of the *Parousia*, and the
reason therefore why in the first instance the "manifestation" is
possible only to those who love him (14.20–3).'[51]

Paul's doctrine of the Body of Christ comes very close to that of
John, for whom the *Parousia* is essentially Christ united to his own.
Both the *Parousia* and the Body of Christ represent that eschatological reality to which the whole work of God is moving. Both
represent our final 'assembling together to him' (II Thess. 2.1), our
ultimate incorporation into the glory and fulness of Christ. There
is, then, but one coming from God and to God. What is ultimately of
significance is not whether or not we prefer the language of John or
the imagery of Paul but rather that we see that coming already
inaugurated, 'whether in the great perfect of the Johannine "It is
finished" (John 19.30) or in that tremendous aorist in which the
Apostle to the gentiles declares (Eph. 1.10) that it was the design of

---

[48] *Jesus and His Coming*, p. 170.   [49] *Ibid.*, p. 173.
[50] *Ibid.*, p. 176; cf. also his booklet of sermons, *Christ Comes In*, London:
Mowbray, 1960.
[51] *Jesus and His Coming*, p. 178.

God, once and for all, in the fulness of time, "to sum up all things" in Christ'.[52]

2. *The Eschatological Community*

The Church is both a community-in-history and a community-in-the-Spirit. It is a community-in-history in that it is the 'covenant people of the new order',[53] the sphere of election into which one enters by baptism (Col. 3.15; Eph. 4.4; and I Cor. 12.13; Gal. 3.27; Rom. 6.3). It is a community-in-the-Spirit because 'that which most decisively marks the Church off from the old Israel, and which stamps it as *the eschatological community*, is its common possession of the Spirit'.[54] It is through the Spirit that we are included in the eschatological community, which is the resurrection body of Christ.[55] The Christian life within this community is set within an intermediate time-period, between the Christ-event and the final consummation of all things in Christ. Although the complete transformation of this body between the Christ-event and the final consummation of all things remains for the future, it is already a reality – 'which is not among the things that are decaying and will finally be dissolved, but is eternal, and ours already in the Spirit, renewing the inward man'. It is both 'a present possession and an ultimate hope'.[56] This community, therefore, lives in the 'age of the overlap',[57] belonging to the new order yet still inhabiting the old. But the decisive events have already occurred: 'At the Resurrection the winning move was played. Thenceforward the issue of the game could not be in doubt. The picture of the "last day" is the representation of the check-mate which *must* follow because in fact it is already contained in the decisive move. The master knows that his opponent must ultimately resign, though he leaves him completely free to continue his moves as he wishes.'[58]

---

[52] *Jesus and His Coming*, p. 185.　　　　　　　　[53] *The Body*, p. 72.
[54] *Idem, loc. cit.* (italics mine).
[55] *Ibid.*, cf. p. 78; cf. also *On Being the Church in the World*, pp. 40–42, 133–134; 'Resurrection in the NT', p. 51; 'Kingdom, Church and Ministry', p. 16; 'The Christian Hope' in *Christian Faith and Communist Faith* (ed. D. M. Mackinnon), London: Macmillan, 1953, pp. 220–222.
[56] *In the End, God . . .* , p. 97.　　　　　　　　[57] *Ibid.*, p. 61.
[58] *Ibid.*, p. 60, n. 1; cf. also 'The Christian Hope', p. 219.

It is through baptism that the substitution of the solidarity of one body by that of another is initiated (Rom. 6). Man as *sarx* is indeed decaying, but man as *soma* is being transformed continually into the Body of Christ. With baptism into the eschatological community a new part of the *soma* of creation, which is made 'for the Lord', begins its release from 'the bondage of corruption' (Rom. 8.21), to which its identification with the *sarx* has doomed it. Robinson insists upon a corporate rather than a purely individual interpretation of I Corinthians 15. It cannot be treated in isolation from the whole corpus of Pauline doctrine. The carrier of the glory (ἔνδοξον) is not the individual but the *Church* (Eph. 5.27), and it is baptism that has rendered the Church capable of this. The powers of life and death have thus been released within the Body. 'And, if the whole is to be interfused, they must operate not simply within each cell as a closed system but between the members. There must be a constant reciprocity of giving and receiving within the Body.'[59]

And just as the Christian hope of resurrection is fundamentally social, so too is it inescapably historical:

> It is a resurrection, not from the body, but of the body. The new creation is not a fresh start, but the old made new – not a νέα but a καινὴ κτίσις (2 Cor. 5.17). It is this very body of sin and death which, transformed, 'must put on incorruption' (1 Cor. 15.54). The building up of the Church is not the gathering of an elect group *out of* the body of history, which is itself signed simply for destruction. It *is* the resurrection body of history itself, the world as its redemption has so far been made effective. . . . The Church is at once the witness to the world of its true nature and the pledge and instrument of its destiny. Those incorporated by God into the Body of His Son are to be 'a kind of firstfruits of his creatures' (James 1.18). So Paul sees the redemption of the body begun in the eschatological community of the Spirit (Rom. 8.11) as the hope ultimately, not only of all men, but of 'the creation itself' (Rom. 8.21). . . . But then the Body of Christ will stand forth, not, as it is now, a world within a world, but as the one solidarity, the restoration of the original image of creation, 'where there cannot be Greek and Jew, circumcision and uncircumcision, barbarian, Scythian, bondman, freeman: but Christ is all, and in all' (Col. 3.10f).[60]

---

[59] *The Body*, p. 82.

[60] *Ibid.*, pp. 82–83; cf. also 'The One Baptism' in *Twelve New Testament Studies*,

The Church is the eschatological community because it is a community-in-the-Spirit, living 'between-the-times' in expectation of the final consummation of all things in Christ. But this is not yet an adequate description because the relationship between Church and Kingdom is conceived of in too static terms. The Church does not simply await the Kingdom; she is indeed the *instrument* of the Kingdom. This concept is central to Robinson's understanding of the Church as the eschatological community and, indeed, to his understanding of the Church's mission in the world.

For Robinson, the Church is the society in which the universal kingship of God in Christ is acknowledged and in which that kingship is, or should be, embodied more fully than in any other section of humanity. It is the instrument by which the rest of creation is to be restored and conformed to the image of the Son, but in fulfilling this instrumental role the Church must resist the 'perennial temptation . . . to equate itself with the kingdom of God on earth, and so to regard itself as the only agent of God in this world'.[61]

Just as the ministry is a function of the Church (we shall examine Robinson's position concerning the ministry of the Church in the following chapter), so the Church is a function of the Kingdom, of the universal Lordship of God in Christ. 'The Kingdom of God, rather even than the People of God, is the controlling category of

---

p. 159, n. 3: 'The baptism of *all men* in the work of Jesus can therefore be described equally as the baptism of *the Church* (e.g., at Pentecost or in Eph. 5.25–7). By that is not meant that only a section of mankind is after all affected – for the Church is, intentionally and eschatologically, the whole of humanity renewed in Christ. Rather, it is only as mankind becomes the Church, and, this side of the Consummation, only in the Church, that what has been universally achieved is individually effective. A man must therefore be incorporated in the Church if the general baptism is to become savingly his own.'

[61] *On Being the Church in the World*, p. 20; cf. also *The Body*, pp. 71–72: 'What is complete in extent has to be made intensively effective: the circle of Christ's kingship must be filled in and filled out. And the agent of that filling is the Church; its function is to extend throughout Christ's redeemed universe the acknowledgment of His victory, "to the intent that now unto the principalities and the powers in the heavenly places might be made known *through the church* the manifold wisdom of God, according to the eternal purpose which he purposed in Christ Jesus our Lord" (Eph. 3.10 f.);' cf. *On Being the Church in the World*, pp. 7–8; *The World that God Loves*, p. 4.

biblical theology for both Old and New Testaments.'[62] The kingship
has been realized once and for all in history by means of Christ's
victory, and it is the task of the Church to translate this victory into
open acknowledgement and moral obedience, 'in order that now,
through the Church, the wisdom of God in all its varied forms might
be made known to the rulers and authorities in the realms of heaven'
(Eph. 3.10). 'Nothing could be more exalted than the doctrine of
the Church which the New Testament presents. . . . Yet ultimately
the New Testament subjects the Church to the Kingdom. This means
that the Church stands always under the judgement of the Kingdom.'[63] To say that the Church lies constantly under the Kingdom
is to relate it dynamically to the two great moments of Christ's
sovereignty over the world: the Cross and the final consummation.
The whole of the Church's ministry derives its character and its
power from these two events. The ministry is a 'making present, a
bringing into effective operation in the here and now, of all that
happened in Palestine, all that will happen at the Parousia. This is
the inner meaning of everything that the Church does – in preaching
and baptism and eucharist, in forgiveness, healing, and discipline.'[64]
The final guarantee of the Church's existence and ministry is
eschatological, that Jesus is and will always be the Lord of history.

Robinson suggests however, that the perspective outlined above
changed in the course of history, that the Church was no longer seen
in subordination to the Kingdom. The Church as the eschatological
community yielded to the Church as the extension of the Incarnation. And in the course of time the hierarchy of values was reversed
completely and the Church became subject not to the Kingdom but
to the Ministry: *ubi episcopus, ibi ecclesia*.[65] This shift in priorities has
had profound and far-reaching repercussions, particularly in such
central ecumenical questions as episcopacy and intercommunion.
Should the trend persist, i.e. should the eschatological community
remain Church-centred rather than Kingdom-centred, Robinson
fears 'that we shall hear the whisper in our soul: "The fruit that you
have longed for is gone from you" (Apoc. 18.14). The forces making

---

[62] 'Kingdom, Church and Ministry', p. 15.
[63] *Ibid.*, p. 16.   [64] *Ibid.*, p. 18.
[65] *Ibid.*, cf. pp. 18–19.

for renewal will have become curved in upon themselves, and all will be lost.'[66]

A CRITICAL ASSESSMENT

1. The Eschatology of the New Testament

'The problem of the *Parousia* is assuredly the most complex and difficult in New Testament exegesis.'[67]

This view of A. Feuillet is amply substantiated by the wide variety of opinions that this question has engendered among the exegetes. The various positions have already been indicated in our account of the state of the question, in which John A. T. Robinson occupies a prominent place. It has been suggested that Robinson's denial of the *Parousia* as a separate and distinct future salvific event is based on certain presuppositions of 'realized' or 'inaugurated eschatology' on the one hand, and on his exegesis of certain key New Testament texts on the other, and that these presuppositions have proved stronger than the exegesis.[68] This is basically the same criticism often levelled against C. H. Dodd who, because of his hypothesis of 'realized eschatology', had had to treat every *Parousia* parable as a crisis parable.[69]

The controlling categories of New Testament eschatology, then, are not *either* futurist *or* realized, but promise *and* fulfilment. They are inseparably united and they are mutually dependent, 'for the promise is made sure by the fulfilment that has already taken place in Jesus, and the fulfilment, being provisional and concealed, loses its quality as a σκάνδαλον only through the knowledge of the promise yet to

---

[66] *The World that God Loves*, p. 4.   [67] 'Parousie', *DBS*, col. 1411.

[68] W. Kümmel, 'Futurische und präsentische Eschatologie in ältesten Urchristentum', *New Testament Studies* 5 (1958–59) 117; cf. also A. J. B. Higgins, *Scottish Journal of Theology* 11 (1958) 316; B. Rigaux, 'La seconde venue de Jésus', *La venue du Messie*, p. 199.

[69] Cf., for example, R. Schnackenburg, *God's Rule and Kingdom*, p. 246. Schnackenburg, in fact, suggests that Robinson's 'inaugurated eschatology' is 'merely a modified version of "realized eschatology"' since it leaves no room for any future expectation after the Resurrection of Jesus' (pp. 246–247). It is difficult, if not impossible, to accept Schnackenburg's observation. Robinson does not deny categorically the element of futurity in the expectation. He only insists that it is now no longer *simply* future but also present. Cf. *Jesus and His Coming*, p. 159; cf. also pp. 180–185.

come'.[70] That this *is* the prevailing dialectic in New Testament eschatology is also accepted by R. Schnackenburg, who writes: 'If we remain faithful to the historical mode of thought of the Bible which moves in the categories of promise and fulfilment, our best way of understanding this presence of the reign of God, preached by Jesus, is as the Messianic era of partial but not complete fulfilment of grace or as the beginning of the eschatological era of salvation, moving always towards its higher level and culmination.'[71]

Central to Robinson's arguments against the *Parousia* as a distinctly and exclusively future salvific event is the notion of a doctrinal development from the preaching of Jesus to the highpoint of futurist eschatology in I and II Thessalonians and finally to its mature culmination in the Fourth Gospel. Critics from every side have rejected such a hypothesis.[72] In attempting to offer some explanation for the obvious fact that the early Christian community cherished a firm belief in the *Parousia*, Robinson – with Glasson[73] – appeals to the influence of certain Old Testament passages, the penetration of apocalyptic notions from the Judaism of the time, and the development of Christology. But this process would have taken place sometime between AD 30 and 50. The small amount of time alone would seem to undermine such an ambitiously-constructed hypothesis. Paul proclaimed this doctrine from the very start (I Thess. 4.15) and the ancient liturgical invocation *maranatha* (I Cor. 16.22) takes us back to the Aramaic-speaking Church of Palestine. The supposed 'break' between Jesus and his Church would have to be placed immediately after the Resurrection, when the disciples became convinced through the apparitions that Jesus still lived and was elevated to the glory of God.[74]

---

[70] W. G. Kümmel, *Promise and Fulfilment*, p. 155.

[71] *God's Rule and Kingdom*, p. 128.

[72] Cf. C. P. Ceroke, *Catholic Biblical Quarterly* 20 (1958) 579–580; V. Taylor, *Expository Times* 69 (1957–8) 104–105; G. R. Beasley-Murray, *Journal of Theological Studies* 10 (1959) 134–140; A. J. B. Higgins, *art. cit.*, pp. 316–318; J. S. Bezzant, *Church Quarterly Review* 159 (1958) 424–427; W. Kümmel, *art. cit.*, p. 120; R. Schnackenburg, *God's Rule and Kingdom*, p. 274.

[73] *The Second Advent*, pp. 151 ff.

[74] B. Rigaux's survey is to be recommended for its examination of the antecedents of Paul's *Parousia*-doctrine in I Thess.; cf. *art. cit.* (in *La venue du Messie*), pp. 178–187.

Another significant feature of Robinson's presentation is the favoured place he accords the Gospel of John, as the most reliable witness of Jesus' eschatological teaching. It would be difficult to disagree with those who have rejected this methodology, for the primacy of John is set forth *a priori* and without proof.[75] In opposing Robinson's attribution of 'inaugurated eschatology' to the Fourth Gospel, Schnackenburg suggests five points which serve to indicate that John has not abandoned the blend of historical and eschatological thought. First, his Gospel presupposes that the era of Jesus and that of the Church follow one another and are mutually related and that this relation is essential to their understanding. Secondly, the Church's missionary situation is certainly implied, for example, in 4.38; 10.16; 11.52; 17.18, 20. This mission never consists in a mere backward glance at salvific acts but always also in a forward striving towards eschatological fulfilment. Thirdly, even though all the graces of salvation are already present in Jesus, John does not move so far from Semitic thinking that he could allow the bodily share in the divine life of glory to lapse. It would, furthermore, be arbitrary to ascribe the texts that speak of resurrection on the Last Day (5.28 ff.; 6.39, 40, 44, 54) to subsequent editing by the Church. The disciple will follow the Risen Lord into heavenly glory, as indicated in 12.26; 14.3; and 17.24. Fourthly, the present judgement neither replaces nor displaces the future judgement; it only anticipates this in the encounter with Jesus. Finally, where Jesus is no longer introduced as speaking during his life on earth but the subject is the glorified Christ, namely in John's first epistle, the eschatological note comes out more strongly (cf. I John 2.28 and 3.2). 'The whole misunderstanding of the Johannine eschatology rests upon an unwarranted "spiritualizing" from which John like all early Christianity is far removed. This does not, however, deny that the Johannine theology has transferred its accent from future to present. . . . What interests us is that John should not be looked upon as an exception who has jettisoned the historical thinking of the early Church or

---

[75] Cf. V. Taylor, *art. cit.*; A. J. B. Higgins, *art. cit.*, especially pp. 317–318; B. Rigaux, *art. cit.*, p. 177; A. Feuillet, 'Parousie', col. 1413; W. Kümmel, *art. cit.*, p. 118.

represented the genuine "eschatological" position of Jesus as against other teachers who misunderstood it.'[76]

We must also add, if only in passing, that Robinson's exegesis of two specific texts – Mark 14.62 and Acts 3.20–21 – has undergone critical, and unfavourable, examination by various reviewers.[77] In agreement with Robinson on Mark 14.62, however, is A. Feuillet.[78]

The various exegetical questions concerning New Testament eschatology are, to a large extent, peripheral to this study of the Church in the thought of Bishop Robinson. Consequently, our 'critical assessment' has been general and superficial, taking into account, for the most part, the views and criticisms of other recognized exegetes and biblical theologians. While exegetical difficulties and differences might remain, it is with some genuine enthusiasm that we can embrace the general eschatological perspective of John A. T. Robinson, as expressed in his study *Jesus and His Coming*: 'That all things were to be consummated in Christ was a hope that no Christian could forgo without jettisoning his faith altogether: to deny it would be to deny the sovereignty of God in Christ over the future as over the past and present.'[79]

[76] *God's Rule and Kingdom*, p. 282; for his discussion on the place of the Fourth Gospel, cf. pp. 278–283. Not all of Schnackenburg's criticisms apply to Bishop Robinson. Nowhere does he suggest that the texts in the Fourth Gospel that speak of the Last Day are subsequent editorial additions. This is Bultmann's position, not Robinson's. Secondly, Robinson has never said that in the Fourth Gospel 'the present judgement replaces or displaces the future judgement'. His discussion of Johannine eschatology in the eighth chapter of *Jesus and His Coming* indicates otherwise. And, finally, Robinson has specifically criticized Dodd's position that the Johannine eschatology represents a 'spiritualizing' of an earlier, cruder eschatology. Cf. 'The New Look on the Fourth Gospel' and 'The Destination and Purpose of the Johannine Epistles'.

[77] Concerning Mark 14.62, cf. M.-E. Boismard, *Revue Biblique* 67 (1960) p. 149; G. R. Beasley-Murray, *art. cit.*, p. 135 f.; B. Rigaux, *art. cit.*, p. 206; R. Schnackenburg, *op. cit.*, p. 172. Concerning Acts 3.20; cf. C. P. Ceroke, *art. cit.*, p. 580; C. S. Morgan, *Journal of Biblical Literature* 78 (1959) 98–99; J. S. Bezzant, *art. cit.*, p. 425 f.; W. Kümmel, *art. cit.*, p. 121.

[78] 'Le Triomphe du Fils de l'homme d'après la déclaration du Christ aux Sanhédrites (Mc xiv, 62; Mt xxvi, 64; Lc xxii, 69)' *passim*.

[79] P. 23.

2. *The Church as the Eschatological Community*

For Bishop Robinson the Church exists 'always and only' as the instrument of the *Kingdom of God*.[80] Despite the fact that Robinson underlines the word 'Kingdom' and not the word 'only', his position is open to some misunderstanding. The Church must always see herself as subject to the rule of God in Christ. To reverse the order of priorities and make the Kingdom subject to the Church would certainly do violence to the witness of the New Testament. However, the word 'only' is ill-advisedly employed because the impression could be left that the bishop fails to take seriously enough the reality of the Church as the Body of Christ. This is definitely *not* his position at all. If it were, it would be strangely contradictory to everything he had written in *The Body*. Yet there *has* been a certain attrition in his doctrine of the Church over the past ten years or so. Robinson has become less concerned with the nature of the Church and more concerned with her mission. He has become disturbed by what he has described as so much 'Church-centred' debate and too little stress on the primacy of the Kingdom.[81] Without retreating from the 'high doctrine' of *The Body*, he has directed his attention in recent years almost exclusively to the question of the Church's mission: her mission of service as the *secular* community (cf. our consideration of *The New Reformation?* and related writings in chapter five) and her mission to preach the gospel to the modern secularized, industrialized and urbanized world (cf. our discussion of *Honest to God* and the concept of the Church as a *missionary* community in chapter six).

The Church is indeed the instrument of the Kingdom. She must preach the gospel relevantly and meaningfully to every age and to every people. 'The Church exists *in* herself, to be sure, but not *for* herself. She exists to serve the world, not to secure privileges and favours from it. She is a minority in the service of the majority.'[82] But she is also, by reason of her very nature, the Body of Christ. It is as the Body of Christ that she is the People of God, the

---

[80] *On Being the Church in the World*, pp. 7–8.

[81] Cf. *The World that God Loves*, p. 4.

[82] R. P. McBrien, 'The Church as the Servant of God', *The Clergy Review* 48 (1963) 410.

eschatological community. It is as the Body of Christ that she is the agent of the Kingdom. It is as the Body of Christ that she acknowledges and extends the Lordship of Christ over all creation.

Particularly influential in this aspect of Robinson's ecclesiology has been Oscar Cullmann, especially his *Christ and Time* and 'The Kingship of Christ and the Church in the New Testament'. The former work is responsible, in large part, for Robinson's concept of the Church as a community-in-history, located 'between-the-times', while the latter study has shaped the bishop's understanding of the interrelationship of Church and Kingdom.

For Cullmann the Church lives between 'this age' and the 'coming age', in a state of 'tension' which 'results from the fact that the mid-point of time no longer falls at the end of the section which lies between the Creation and the *Parousia;* it now falls rather in the middle of this period, so that the present of the Church already lies in the new age, and yet is still before the *Parousia,* and so before the actual end time.'[83] Given this peculiar location in the context of salvation-history the Church becomes 'the place where the Spirit, this feature of the eschatological period, is already at work as "earnest", as "firstfruits" '.[84] This vision is certainly consonant with the recent teaching of the Second Vatican Council, which we have already outlined.[85]

Robinson's unhappiness with the shift of emphasis in theology from the Church as the eschatological community of the Messiah to the notion of the Church as the extension of the Incarnation,[86] finds an echo in E. Schillebeeckx:

> Sacramental encounter with the living Christ in the Church is therefore, in virtue of the historical mysteries of Christ's life, the actual beginning of eschatological salvation on earth.
> To say that the Church in her sacraments is a prolongation of the earthly life of Christ appears therefore to be an elliptical or insufficient statement of the case. Certainly the Church in her visibility prolongs the function of the earthly visibility which Christ once enjoyed. But the Passover brought about a change of emphasis; Christ *lives* now, at this moment. His glorious body continues to fulfil the function it had

---

[83] *Christ and Time*, p. 145.　　　　　　[84] *Ibid.*, p. 155.
[85] Cf. pp. 53–55 of this chapter.
[86] 'Kingdom, Church and Ministry', p. 19.

during his earthly life. But because this sign of Jesus' lifegiving redemptive act has become invisible to us, this body of the Lord is prolonged in a form which is visible on earth – in the sacramental Church. In this sense, the Church is a prolongation primarily of the heavenly Christ, and therefore it prolongs the function of the earthly body of Jesus. . . . 'Christ is the Lord, sitting at God's right hand', is the fundamental confession of faith in both past and future *parousia*.[87]

In summary, therefore, our basis of agreement with the ecclesiological perspective of John A. T. Robinson is far wider than is our area of disagreement. He is correct in insisting that the Church as the eschatological community is a community set 'between-the-times' and a community of the Spirit. He is correct in underlining the subordinate and instrumental role of Church to Kingdom of God. We must disagree, however, with his judgement regarding the precise nature of the 'end-time', specifically in his rejection of the *Parousia* (with the qualifications that he makes) and in his advocacy of a position of universalism.[88]

In the following chapter we shall consider two corollaries of what has been discussed thus far in chapters two and three; namely, Robinson's concept of ministry in the Church and his understanding of the nature and role of the liturgy. Our discussion of the liturgy especially will provide a transition from Part I to Part II of this study, for the liturgy of the Church reflects both the nature of the Church as Body of Christ and as the eschatological community, and also her essential mission of service and preaching.

[87] *Christ the Sacrament of Encounter with God*, London: Sheed & Ward (Stagbook), 1963, pp. 74–75.

[88] Cf. *In the End, God* . . . , chapter 9, pp. 108–123, and 'Universalism – Is it Heretical?', *Scottish Journal of Theology* 2 (1949) 139–155; For two replies from Protestant theologians, cf. R. H. Fuller, *Theology* 54 (1951) 269–270, and T. P. Torrance, 'Universalism or Election?' *Scottish Journal of Theology* 2 (1949) 310–318.

4

THE MINISTRY AND LITURGY
OF THE CHURCH

THE Body of Christ is not a static community but a community-in-history and a community-in-the-Spirit. The Church exists not for her own sake but for the sake of the Kingdom. As such the Church has a mission to fulfil, a mission whose source is the Holy Spirit (cf. Acts 2.33) and whose task is to extend the reign of Christ over all creation, to bring the universe into a unity in Christ (Eph. 1.10). This is a mission which grows out of her nature as the Body of Christ and the eschatological community, or the People of God.

All of this can be said of the Church because it can first be said of Christ himself, for the Church is in Christ as a sacrament of the intimate union with God and of the unity of the whole human race.[1] Christ is 'the image of the invisible God; his is the primacy over all created things' (Col. 1.15). But the Word became flesh and came to dwell among us (John 1.14), for although 'the divine nature was his from the first, yet he did not think to snatch at equality with God, but made himself nothing, assuming the nature of a slave' (Phil. 2.6–7). The Son of Man came not for his own sake, 'not . . . to be served but to serve, and to surrender his life as a ransom for many' (Mark 10.45). The Christology of the New Testament is a strongly *functional* Christology.[2]

[1] Cf. Concilium Vaticanum Secundum, sess. III, *Constitutio dogmatica de Ecclesia*, I, 1: 'Cum autem Ecclesia sit in Christo veluti sacramentum seu signum et instrumentum intimae cum Deo unionis totiusque generis humani unitatis, naturam missionemque suam universalem . . . pressius fidelibus suis et mundo universo declarare intendit.' Cf. also E. Schillebeeckx, *Christ the Sacrament of Encounter with God*, chapter 2, pp. 55 ff.

[2] Cf. O. Cullmann, *The Christology of the New Testament*, pp. 1–10, *et passim*.

It is within this theological context that we initiate our discussion of Bishop Robinson's understanding of the ministry and liturgy of the Church. For the ministry is a function of the Church and the liturgy is the summit and source of her life, reflecting her true nature as the Body of Christ and the eschatological community and pointing toward her proper mission in the world. As such, this aspect of our investigation should shed further light on his notion of the Church as the Body of Christ and as the eschatological community and should set in clearer relief his most recently expressed views on the mission of the Church as presented in *Honest to God* and *The New Reformation?*

Since this discussion represents but a corollary of the two preceding chapters and occupies a transitional place in this study, the treatment will be less extensive and the methodology will differ accordingly. We shall present Bishop Robinson's position under three general headings, analysing each in the light of three major ecclesiological constitutions of the Second Vatican Council: *De Sacra Liturgia* (second session), *De Ecclesia* (third session), and *De Ecumenismo* (third session). The three general divisions of this chapter will include: the interrelationship of ministry and liturgy in the Church, with particular reference to the problem of intercommunion; the nature and role of the ministry; and the nature and place of the liturgy.

THE INTERRELATIONSHIP OF MINISTRY AND LITURGY IN THE CHURCH

That Bishop Robinson posits an intimate connection between the ministry and the liturgy of the Church is evident in his own definition of the Christian ministry: 'For the Christian ministry is no other than the ministry, the liturgy, of Christ Himself as He channels through preaching and sacrament, through forgiveness and healing, the continuous creation of the New World wrought on Easter Day.'[3] The instrument of this ministry, this liturgy, of Christ is his own Resurrection Body, the Church. Thus, the Christian ministry is 'first and last and all the time a function of the Body of Christ' and the vocation to the priesthood in the Church 'cannot be sustained,

[3] 'Kingdom, Church and Ministry', p. 13.

exercised or prepared for except within the context of the Worshipping Community'.[4] The close relationship is dramatized even more pointedly in his discussion of the episcopacy, in an essay written two years after his own consecration: 'The office of a bishop is as much a liturgical one as anything else. As Ignatius insisted, the bishop is the centre of unity because he is the breaker of Bread that makes us one. In this capacity, he is the *persona* of the local Church and its link with the universal Church, the focus and expression of its catholicity and apostolicity.'[5]

The ministry, then, is a function of the Church and, as such, is subordinate to the Church. But it is a function of the Church in her *priestly* character, i.e. 'as the worshipping and as the witnessing community'.[6] This dual task is outlined in I Peter 2.5, 9; namely, 'to offer spiritual sacrifices acceptable to God through Jesus Christ', and 'to proclaim the triumphs of him who has called you out of darkness into his marvellous light'. This same epistle indicates that it is the whole Church which is 'a royal priesthood' (I Peter 2.9), and so the celebrant at every Eucharist is not the priest (who is more properly called the 'president' of the assembly) but the whole congregation of the People of God.[7] To deny this fact, practically as well as theoretically, is to invite further and more serious ecclesiological aberrations, for 'liturgy is normative of ministry' and 'a clericalized liturgy means a clericalized apostolate'.[8]

The theological perspective outlined briefly in the preceding paragraphs is very similar to that of the Second Vatican Council, both in its constitution *De Sacra Liturgia* and in its later constitution, *De Ecclesia*. In the former document the liturgy is presented as 'an exercise of the priestly office of Jesus Christ', now 'performed by the mystical body of Jesus Christ, that is, by the head and his members'.[9] *De Ecclesia* also basically agrees with Robinson's position, but introduces an important distinction which Bishop Robinson, in none of his writings, has been willing to make; namely, that the common

[4] 'The Theological College in a Changing World', *Theology* 55 (1952) 207.
[5] 'A New Model of Episcopacy', in *Bishops: What they are and what they do*, p. 128.
[6] *On Being the Church in the World*, p. 76.   [7] *Ibid.*, cf. p. 80.
[8] *Liturgy Coming to Life*, p. vii (new preface to the second edition).
[9] Concilium Vaticanum Secundum, sess. II, *Constitutio de Sacra Liturgia*, I, 7.

priesthood of the faithful and the ministerial or hierarchical priest-hood differ not only in degree but also in essence. Yet they are certainly related one with the other because 'each of them in its own special way is a participation in the one priesthood of Christ. The ministerial priest, by the sacred power he enjoys, teaches and rules the priestly people acting in the person of Christ, makes present the eucharistic sacrifice and offers it to God in the name of all the people. But the faithful, in virtue of their royal priesthood, join in the offering of the Eucharist.'[10] Finally, 'it is through the sacraments and the exercise of the virtues that the sacred nature and organic structure of the priestly community is brought into existence'.[11]

The harmony between John A. T. Robinson and Vatican II becomes slightly strained when the bishop directs his attention to the very pressing question of *intercommunion*. Liturgy and ministry clearly intersect at this delicate point. 'The more convinced we are of the centrality of the Eucharist to our own Church life,' he writes, 'the more insistent is the question of intercommunion when we work and meet together. The limits to non-sacramental co-operation are reached very much sooner in a generation brought up on the litur-gical movement.'[12]

Bishop Robinson has addressed himself to this problem in three separate essays over the past decade: 'Intercommunion and Con-celebration' (1957), 'Episcopacy and Intercommunion' (1959), and *The Church of England and Intercommunion* (Prism pamphlet, 1962).[13] His position remains substantially the same throughout.

He describes the current climate of opinion in terms of two oppos-ing points of view: those who look to intercommunion as the *expression* of unity achieved, and those who regard it also as a *means* to the achievement of that unity. 'The presupposition of the first',

[10] II, 10; cf. also Pius XII, Alloc. *Magnificate Dominum*, Nov. 2, 1954. *AAS* 46 (1954) p. 669; Litt. Encycl. *Mediator Dei*, Nov. 20, 1947. *AAS* 39 (1947) p. 555; Pius XI, Litt. Encycl. *Miserentissimus Redemptor*, May 8, 1928. *AAS* 20 (1928) p. 171 f.; Pius XII, Alloc. *Vous nous avez*, Sept. 22, 1956. *AAS* 48 (1956) p. 714.

[11] *De Ecclesia*, II, 11.

[12] *The Church of England and Intercommunion*, London: Prism Pamphlet, no. 2, 1962, p. 3.

[13] The first two articles are reprinted in *On Being the Church in the World*, chapter VI, pp. 96–100, and chapter VII, pp. 101–109.

he remarks, 'is that intercommunion is impossible until there is a unity, alike of faith and of order, which it can genuinely express. The presupposition of the second is that intercommunion is one of the most powerful means towards such union, and as such must not be denied even now.'[14] The first position would be that of the Anglo-Catholics primarily,[15] and the second that of the Evangelicals and others.[16] Once again Bishop Robinson stands against the Anglo-Catholic opinion, but without compromising his own High-Church theology.

The Eucharist does *not* express the empirical unity of the Church, whether now or in the future. Rather, it brings to us, and brings upon us, the perfect unity of Christ, 'both that primal unity which is ours in the finished work of Christ and that eschatological unity of the one new Man made whole in him'. 'Every Eucharist', he continues, 'is the *anamnesis* of the one and a forestallment of the other. In each case it makes present and brings to us a unity which empirically *does not exist* except in a gravely distorted reflection. The mistake arises when we allow our attitude to intercommunion to be determined, not by reference to *this* unity, but solely by reference to the greater degree of empirical unity which we see ahead of us: *when* the greater unity does come, or *if* thereby it can come, then intercommunion becomes justified.'[17]

But, in point of fact, this future hope cannot be realized during the earthly pilgrimage of the Church. The Eucharist will always be presenting and anticipating a unity which empirically does not exist. 'The sole test is not whether or not we are sufficiently united

[14] *On Being the Church in the World*, p. 96.

[15] Cf., for example, A. M. Ramsey, *The Gospel and the Catholic Church* (2nd ed.), London: Longmans, 1956, p. 105; E. L. Mascall, *Christ, the Christian, and the Church*. London: Longmans, 1946. This was always the traditional opinion of the Lambeth Conferences; thus, in 1930 it resolved (Res. n. 42) that 'intercommunion should be the goal of, rather than a means to, the restoration of unity'. By 1948 a distinction was made between full and *partial* intercommunion, with the Church of South India especially in mind (Part II, p. 48; cf. also 1958, Part II, p. 28). Cf. also D. Paton, *Anglicans and Unity*, London: Mowbray, 1962, pp. 94 ff. (The reports of the Lambeth Conferences are published by SPCK, London, in the same years in which they were held.)

[16] The best representative of this position is S. L. Greenslade, *Schism in the Early Church*, London: SCM Press, 1953, cf. p. 210.

[17] *On Being the Church in the World*, pp. 96–97.

to *express our* unity by "coming together to one place", but whether we are united enough to *bear Christ's* unity by receiving to ourselves and upon ourselves what we are not – or, rather, what we are and fail to be. For by eating and drinking we deliberately take to ourselves the one Body which we find we cannot be.'[18]

We are confronted, then, with two basic principles: (1) we cannot communicate until there is a unity to express; and (2) the Eucharist *creates* us as the one Body we find we cannot be. Bishop Robinson insists that 'neither of these principles must be emphasized to the exclusion of the other'.[19] 'Dare we say *together*, "Come, Lord Jesus!" Or dare we go on saying it *apart?* In which lies the greater sin? We must always be prepared to ask both questions with equal seriousness – and not simply the first.'[20]

The problem of ministry is usually interposed at this point. Can we break bread together without a single or mutually recognized ministry? Robinson is impatient with such a concern because it seems to subordinate the Church to the ministry rather than the ministry to the Church, which is the only true order.[21] His own solution to the problem is an admittedly temporary one: concelebration. In lieu of this, the Christian communities are prone to absolve themselves from thinking out the theological conditions in which intercommunion becomes less sinful than separate communions.

In calling for concelebration by a plurality of ministries, Bishop Robinson is not suggesting that the schism between the various Christian ministries is not 'a major, perhaps the major, rift in the Body which causes us to eat judgement when we feed upon the undivided Body'. On the contrary, the very presence of these divided ministers is a reminder, not a cloaking, of the judgement involved. 'But at least it does open the way for mercy to rejoice over judgement. And that mercy is the supreme divine reality to which our oneness in Christ, despite our disunity as Churches, is the constant and marvellous testimony.'[22]

---

[18] *On Being the Church in the World*, p. 97.
[19] *Idem., loc. cit.*   [20] *Ibid.*, p. 98.
[21] *Idem, loc. cit.*; cf. also 'Kingdom, Church and Ministry', *passim.*
[22] *On Being the Church in the World*, p. 100.

In a second article (1959), Bishop Robinson considers the problem of intercommunion with the episcopacy in mind specifically. He insists once again, with St Ignatius of Antioch, that the bishop must be the centre and focus of unity in any given place of the one, catholic Church, 'or he is nothing worth contending for'. 'Let us go all out to achieve a single ministry which is truly catholic and which all acknowledge,' he continues. 'Let us beware, as a supposed half-way house to that, of multiplying episcopates. If the bishop is the focus of the catholic Church in any one place, then there cannot be two bishops any more than two catholic Churches.'[23]

That having been stated, Robinson proceeds to suggest that the episcopacy is often commended on the wrong grounds – not as the basis of unity, as outlined above, but as the condition of intercommunion, 'as a gimmick for validating sacraments'.[24] Over against this view, he reiterates his position that intercommunion is not only justified but even imperative when a situation is reached in which it becomes more sinful *not* to break a common loaf than to do so. But intercommunion without any real desire for *union* may be just as sinful as to refrain from doing so. And this, he feels, is the situation which exists in the majority of the parishes in England, where the congregations of different denominations are perfectly content to go on in their separate ways. 'Indiscriminate intercommunion in these circumstances would be sin, *and would continue to be so even if the other denomination were episcopal.*'[25] In summary: intercommunion is 'the

---

[23] *On Being the Church in the World*, p. 103; cf. also 'A New Model of Episcopacy', pp. 137–138: 'To be consecrated a bishop in the Church of God has indeed in this age more far-reaching implications than in any generation since the Reformation. . . . For a bishop, wherever he is, is called to represent the wholeness of the catholic Church to its divided parts, to be the creative focus of its coming unity. That is why *deliberately to create parallel episcopates* (for the sake of inter-communion) as the Interim Report on the Anglican–Methodist Conversations proposed, looks, the more one views it, a very horrible thing. It is to shatter the episcopate as the focus of unity, in order to use it for the time being as a means of validating sacraments. Let us at all costs not divide the episcopate. For it is a visible token of unity, a pledge of the coming great Church. Already in a real sense it belongs to us all. But "what it might become for us and our children" can and will only be known in its fulness as it embraces the *episcope* of all Christ's scattered flock.'

[24] *On Being the Church in the World*, p. 105.

[25] *Idem, loc. cit.*

means to union and not merely . . . the fruit of it'.[26] 'Let the one loaf in the one place, the one common Christian life, *despite* our divisions on order, be the spiritual reality that compels us to a common structure and a common episcopacy.'[27]

The arguments of both these articles are resumed and reaffirmed in his most recent essay on intercommunion (1962). He continues to reject both the rigid presuppositions of the Anglo-Catholics and the imprecise and unbiblical advocacies of the Evangelicals. Casual intercommunion without any thirst for unity is still a very dangerous procedure (cf. I Cor. 11.29), yet the Eucharist has the power to recreate us as the one Body because of the one loaf (I Cor. 10.17). 'The Anglican witness has concentrated so heavily on the first truth, and the Free Church witness has related the grace of intercommunion so inadequately to union, that it is necessary to emphasize the implications of St Paul's second great truth.'[28] The Free Churches cannot expect Anglicans simply to renounce the necessity of the episcopacy where it can be had, yet Free Church ministries are visibly blessed by the Spirit as real means of grace. Anglicans, in Robinson's view, must eventually declare the rightness of inter-communion and that it should be mutual. The Anglican tendency is to assume that as long as there is an episcopally ordained celebrant no other theological issue matters very much.

In conclusion, he writes:

> To ask Anglicans to say that efficacy *equals* validity, and that there-fore Free Church ministries are, as it were, justified by their works, is again to ask them to renounce convictions conscientiously held. To say, on the other hand, that validity is all is to risk being found fighting against the Holy Ghost. Let us admit that full validity for all our ministries is only the fruit of union, and must wait upon it. But mean-while let us acknowledge the relevance here, as Bishop Newbigin pleads (*The Reunion of the Church*, esp. ch. VI), of the principle of justification, not by works, but by faith – faith in the one Spirit who is even now at work through us all and who wills to bring us into unity not by our merits but by the sheer grace of God. When we are prepared to accept each other as Christ accepted us, not on the basis of what as denominations we have to contribute but for what he has the power

[26] *On Being the Church in the World*, p. 107.   [27] *Ibid.*, p. 108.
[28] *The Church of England and Intercommunion*, p. 8.

to make of us, then, as in South India, mercy can triumph over judgement, and all things, validity and whatever else is necessary, can be
added to us.[29]

Bishop Robinson's discussion of the problem of intercommunion
confirms the outline of his ecclesiology that has been sketched thus
far in this study. His doctrine of the Church is High-Church without
being Anglo-Catholic, comprehensive without being compromising.
He is impatient with questions of ecclesiastical order because the
Church is higher than the ministry, and the Kingdom higher than
the Church. True to the English empirical tradition, he is unim-
pressed with abstractions. *De facto*, the Church is *not* united; unity is
but an eschatological goal and hope, something for which we are
bound to strive, with the knowledge that the Spirit alone can grant it.

Such a perspective does not correspond perfectly with that of the
De Ecumenismo decree of the Second Vatican Council. In this document the Eucharist is presented as the sacrament by which the unity
of the Church is both signified and made a reality (*et significatur et
efficitur*).[30] Only after the various obstacles to perfect ecclesiastical
communion have been gradually overcome will all Christians be able
to gather in a common celebration of the Eucharist and to gather into
a single Church in that unity which Christ bestowed on his Church
from the beginning. 'We believe', the Council proclaims, 'that this
unity subsists in the Catholic Church as something she can never
lose, and we hope that it will continue to increase until the end of
time.'[31] And so worship in common (*communicatio in sacris*) is 'not to
be considered as a means to be used indiscriminately for the restoration of Christian unity'.[32] Thus far the Council appears to adopt the
somewhat rigid position of the Anglo-Catholics from which Robinson
has clearly dissociated himself. Yet the Council goes on to indicate
that there are two main principles governing the practice of such
common worship, and the similarity to Robinson's approach is
striking: 'first, the bearing witness to the unity of the Church; and,
secondly, the sharing in the means of grace. Witness to the unity of
the Church generally forbids common worship to Christians, but the

[29] *The Church of England and Intercommunion*, p. 11.
[30] Concilium Vaticanum Secundum, Sess. III, *Decretum de Ecumenismo*, I, 2.
[31] *Ibid.*, II, 4; cf. also II, 3.   [32] *Ibid.*, II, 8.

grace to be had from it sometimes commends the practice.'[33] Still
further on, the Council especially commends the practice of intercommunion with the Eastern Orthodox Churches who 'although
separated from us, yet possess true sacraments and, above all,
apostolic succession, the priesthood and the Eucharist, whereby
they are linked with us in the closest intimacy. Therefore some
worship in common, given suitable circumstances and the approval
of church authority, is not merely possible but to be encouraged.'[34]
Even though the Council does not adopt or even mention the solution
suggested by Bishop Robinson, namely concelebration, the agreement *in principle* seems obvious enough.

THE NATURE AND ROLE OF MINISTRY IN THE CHURCH

As we have already noted,[35] Bishop Robinson identifies the
Christian ministry with 'the ministry, the liturgy, of Christ Himself
as He channels through preaching and sacrament, through forgiveness and healing, the continuous creation of the New World wrought
on Easter Day'. But Robinson insists less on this descriptive definition
than he does on the fundamental relationship that exists between
the ministry and the Church; namely, that the ministry is always
subordinate to the Church and can never be its precondition.[36]

The ministry is the ministry of Christ only in so far as it is the

---

[33] *Decretum de Ecumenismo*, II, 8.

[34] *Ibid.*, III, 15. Just as Bishop Robinson's views on intercommunion can, in
principle, be reconciled with those of the Second Vatican Council, so, too, is
there much room for agreement with regard to the question of the empirical
unity of the Church. Robinson insists that there is no *de facto* empirical unity to
express, whereas the Council teaches that the unity of the Church is both
expressed and signified, and subsists even now in the Catholic Church. Yet, in
another paragraph (I, 3) the Council grants *real communion*, though it is *imperfect*,
to all who believe in Christ and are truly baptized. Thus: 'Hi enim qui in
Christum credunt et baptismum rite receperunt in quadam cum Ecclesia
catholica communione, etsi non perfecta, constituuntur.' They are members of
the Church, but by reason of an imperfect relationship of communion. Therefore,
empirically at least, the Church does not possess *perfect* unity.

[35] Cf. p. 74; cf. also *On Being the Church in the World*, pp. 79–81, for Robinson's
description of the threefold task of the Christian ministry, namely, liturgy,
absolution, and healing.

[36] Cf., for example, 'Kingdom, Church and Ministry,' pp. 15, 17, and 22.

ministry of the Church. 'All that is said of the ministry in the NT [*sic*] is said not of individuals nor of some apostolic college or "essential ministry" but of the whole Body, whatever the differentiation of function within it. This follows because the whole life of Christ is given to the Church to be possessed *in solidum:* the Spirit, the New Life, the Priesthood, everything, belongs to each only as it belongs to all.'[37] This is a central notion in Robinson's doctrine of the ministry and is one that he frequently reaffirms throughout his writings.[38] He underlines this theological judgement by introducing the distinction between the priesthood of the Old Testament and the priesthood of the New Law. In the former instance the priesthood was always *vicarious*, in that the priest did for the people what they could not do for themselves. There was but one priestly tribe, not twelve. But in the New Testament this kind of division, according to Robinson, was 'utterly abolished'.[39] Christ alone is High Priest and Mediator between God and man and there is no priestly caste within his Body. The entire Body is a royal priesthood (I Peter 2.9) and every member has his share in that priesthood by virtue of his baptism. The ordained ministry in the New Law is not a vicarious one but a *representative* one. The ministry that the ordained exercise is always the ministry of the whole Body, 'not of course, the ministry of the Body apart from the Head, as if their authority came simply from below, but neither of the Head apart from the Body, but of the Head working through the Body'.[40]

More specifically:

> What is given to the ordained minister is formal authority to preach and proclaim in the name of the whole Church what every member has not only the right but the duty to proclaim. He is given formal authority to exercise the ministry of reconciliation and forgiveness which belongs by right to every member of the healing community. He is given formal authority to lead and preside at the celebration

[37] *Ibid.*, p. 14.
[38] Cf. *On Being the Church in the World*, pp. 74–75; *The Body: A Study in Pauline Theology*, pp. 68–71; 'Taking the Lid off the Church's Ministry,' in *New Ways with the Ministry*, London: Faith Press, 1960, p. 10; 'A New Model of Episcopacy', p. 128; and 'The Ministry and the Laity', in *Layman's Church*, London: Lutterworth Press, 1963, p. 14.
[39] 'The Ministry and the Laity', p. 14.   [40] *Ibid.*, p. 15.

which is the con-celebration of the whole people of God. For in this sense every celebration is a lay celebration. The celebrant is the entire *laos*, of which the bishop or presbyter is 'the president'.[41]

It should be added, however, that Robinson is careful to criticize and set himself apart from the Reformers' concept of 'the priesthood of all believers'. In practice, the bishop observes, it was often understood as 'the priesthood of *each* believer'; 'just as Luther's profoundly biblical teaching on the freedom of a Christian man was perverted to imply that every man was his own pope'.[42] On the contrary, the priesthood of Christ is vested in the people of God *as a Body*. It is held *in solidum*.

And just as the ministry has an essential relationship to the Church as the Body of Christ, so too must it be viewed in the light of Christian eschatology, i.e. in relation to the Church as the eschatological community. Robinson is emphatic on this point: 'We shall not get our theology of the Church and the Ministry right until we get our eschatology right.'[43] For the failure to relate the Church properly to the Kingdom issues also in the failure to relate the ministry properly to the Church.

Central to the notion of the Church as the eschatological community are both the historical dimension (i.e. a community-in-history) and the possession of – or, perhaps better, *by* – the Holy Spirit (i.e. a community-in-the-Spirit). Bishop Robinson notes the relationship of the ministry to the aforementioned in the following terms: 'Indeed, there is an essential connection between the solidarity of the priesthood and the solidarity of the Spirit in the life of the Church. For one of the truly revolutionary claims and characteristics

[41] *Ibid.*, p. 14; cf. Bishop Robinson's practical suggestions to eliminate what he calls the 'clergy line', the 'professional line', and the 'sex line' in the Christian ministry: *The New Reformation?*, pp. 55–60; 'Taking the Lid off the Church's Ministry,' pp. 10–21; 'The Ministry and the Laity,' p. 14 *et passim*. Agreement with these views is expressed on the Catholic side by the *De Ecclesia* constitution of the Second Vatican Council (IV, 31) which grants that 'those in holy orders can at times be engaged in secular activities, and even have a secular profession'. On the question of the ordination of women to the priesthood, cf. G. Heinzelmann, 'The Priesthood and Women' (tr. W. Kramer), *Commonweal* 81 (1965) 504–508; and M. Daly, 'A Built-in Bias', *ibid.*, pp. 508–511.

[42] *On Being the Church in the World*, p. 75.

[43] 'Kingdom, Church and Ministry', p. 17.

of the early Church was what it called "the common ownership", the *koinonia*, of Holy Spirit. Hitherto the "holy" had been defined as that which was *not* "common" – and the "holy" was the sphere of the priest. With the communalization of the holy went the communalization of the priesthood.'[44] And, as for the historical dimension, the ministry is set 'between-the-times': between the salvific events initiated at Calvary and the consummation of all things at the end. 'For the bishop is set in the Church also as a sign of the End, a pledge of the coming *episcope* or visitation of Christ. He represents in his office a gathering into one which is *not yet* achieved; and under God, it may be given to him to be not only the sacramental sign but an effective instrument of that unity.'[45]

The episcopacy, essentially related as it is both to the Church as the Body of Christ and to the Church as the eschatological community, occupies an important place in Robinson's ecclesiology. The New Testament doctrine of the episcopacy illustrates the fundamental polarity which characterizes the whole Christian ministry. 'The *episcope* of the Church (that is, of Christ · in His Church) is that which stands between and mediates to this present age, the *episcope*, the visitation, of God to His people in Christ's first coming and in His last.'[46] Until the great day of visitation occurs, the *episcope* must exercise *oversight* in the Church (cf. I Peter 5.2). This function is to be continually exercised until the chief Shepherd himself be manifested (I Peter 5.4), who is himself the *Episcopos* of men (I Peter 2.25). The episcopacy, and indeed the entire ministry of the Church, is 'validated' by the mighty acts of God. The final guarantee lies in the assurance that in the end it will still be 'this same Jesus' crowned Lord of history and not another. It is thus in

---

[44] *On Being the Church in the World*, p. 76; cf. also 'Kingdom, Church and Ministry,' p. 18: 'The ministry of the Church is the present ministry "between the times" of the Christ who has come and will come. This ministry derives its character and its power from these two mighty acts. It is a making present, a bringing into effective operation in the here and now, of all that happened in Palestine, all that will happen at the Parousia. This is the inner meaning of everything that the Church does – in preaching and baptism and eucharist, in forgiveness, healing and discipline.'

[45] 'A New Model of Episcopacy', p. 137.

[46] 'Kingdom, Church and Ministry', p. 18.

terms of eschatology that the Church and its ministry receive their
ultimate validation (cf. Matt. 26.18 f.; Luke 12.32; 22.29 f.). When
this New Testament perspective was lost, the Church and her
ministry was set 'adrift from its anchor of hope' and she 'grasped the
life-line of historical succession'. 'Shorn of its guarantee in the
Kingdom,' Robinson suggests, 'it sought its title-deeds in the
Ministry. The episcopate, instead of being an organ of its life,
became the hall-mark of its very existence, "the authentic guarantee
of its claim to be the Body of Christ among men" (K. E. Kirk, *The
Apostolic Ministry*, p. 46): *ubi episcopus, ibi ecclesia*.'[47]

It is within this particular biblical frame of reference that Robinson
criticizes the Anglo-Catholic posture, which he describes as an
'historical curiosity'.[48] The Anglo-Catholics believe they belong to
the true Church because their orders are valid – again, it is a case of
the Church being subordinated to the ministry, rather than *vice versa*.
Robinson does not argue, however, against the importance of
continuity, or of the historic episcopate, or of apostolic succession.
'A Church without continuity in time', he remarks, 'is as sinful and
broken as a Church without unity in space.'[49] Without the historic
episcopate the Church in fact cannot be fully one, catholic, or
apostolic.[50] What he is concerned to deny is only that particular

[47] 'Kingdom, Church and Ministry', p. 19.

[48] *Ibid.*, p. 21; cf. also pp. 11 f., and 15; *The Church of England and Intercommunion*, pp. 7, 10–11.

[49] 'Kingdom, Church and Ministry', p. 21; cf. also *On Being the Church in the
World*, p. 100; *The Church of England and Intercommunion*, pp. 7, 10–11. This question
has been discussed already in the first section of this chapter.

[50] Robinson's views on the monepiscopacy are worth noting here: 'Everything
turns on how one understands monepiscopacy. If by this is meant monarchical
episcopacy, in the sense that the bishop is the sole repository of *episcope* within his
diocese, then the suffragan is a mere substitute, and in the presence of his diocesan
an embarrassing anomaly. But if by monepiscopacy one means that the bishop
is the centre and expression of an *episcope* belonging to Christ in his whole Church,
then it can be focused in him without being confined to him. It can be exercised
corporately, both in the sense that many of the functions of *episcope* may be
performed by men not in episcopal orders, and in the sense that the local
episcopate, headed by the diocesan, may itself be a corporate entity. On this
view, not only would any member of the diocesan episcopate be empowered to
act in the name of the principal, but when together it would normally act
corporately, e.g. at ordinations. . . . Nor, I believe, shall we be able to commend
episcopacy ecumenically unless we can demonstrate within our own system

interpretation of the episcopate which would automatically unchurch any part of the Body which for historical reasons had failed to preserve it. This is equivalent to saying that the episcopacy is of the *plene esse* of the Church. '*It is not what makes the Church the Church – so that in exclusion from it everything falls to the ground. But in repudiation of it the Church can never express the plenitude of its Being as the one Body of Christ in history.*'[51]

In summary: Bishop Robinson views the ministry as a function of, and subordinate to, the Church. It is to be understood as essentially *service*: 'And this conception of the ministry, which is after all the papal conception of the ministry (for it is the proud title of the Pope that he is the *servus servorum Dei*) is, I believe, the clue to the whole revolution. For we can never hold too high a doctrine of the ordained ministry if we really see it, as the New Testament does, as the ministry of the servant, in direct extension of the ministry of the Son of Man who came not to be ministered unto but to minister.'[52]

It is impossible to disagree with the view that the priesthood of Christ is conferred upon, and exercised by, the whole Church, the Body of Christ. For the liturgy, which is the supreme expression of Christ's priesthood, is the worship of the entire Body of Christ, Head and members.[53] For all the baptized constitute a holy priesthood (cf. Rev. 1.6; 5.9–10; I Peter 2.9).[54] And this priesthood, this ministry, is a *service* – in direct extension of the ministry of the Son of Man and the Servant of God (cf. Mark 10.45). This is clearly the teaching of the Second Vatican Council as well.[55]

But Bishop Robinson excludes too readily the notion of the *vicarious* priesthood. The priesthood of the faithful, of the People of God as

that monepiscopacy and corporate episcopacy are not mutually exclusive' ('A New Model of Episcopacy,' p. 133, n. 1); cf. also 'Kingdom, Church and Ministry,' p. 21, n. 1.

[51] 'Kingdom, Church and Ministry', p. 22.
[52] 'The Ministry and the Laity', p. 17; cf. also H. Küng, *The Council and Reunion* (tr. C. Hastings), London: Sheed & Ward, 1961, p. 191; Y. M.-J. Congar, *Power and Poverty in the Church* (tr. J. Nicholson), London: Geoffrey Chapman, 1964, *passim*; R. McBrien, 'The Church as the Servant of God,' *Clergy Review* 48 (1963) 403–416.
[53] Concilium Vaticanum Secundum, sess. II, *Constitutio de Sacra Liturgia*, I, 7.
[54] *De Ecclesia*, II, 10; IV, 31.
[55] Cf. *De Ecclesia*, III, 18, 20, 26, 28, 29, *et passim*.

such, differs not only in degree but in *essence* from the priesthood of Holy Order. Though each is a participation in the one priesthood of Christ, the ordained priest, by the sacred power he enjoys, 'teaches and rules the priestly people, makes present (*conficit*) the Eucharistic sacrifice in the person of Christ (*in persona Christi*), and offers it to God in the name of the entire People of God (*nomine totius populi Dei*)'.[56] The notion of vicarious, and not *exclusively* representative, priestly power is also evident in the Council's teaching on the episcopate.[57]

Robinson is correct, of course, in insisting upon the unity of the episcopate, but it is certainly not surprising that he should ignore the papacy as 'a permanent and visible principle and foundation' of episcopal unity in faith and communion.[58] To ask him to accept this and the whole corpus of Catholic doctrine on the papacy is to require a renunciation of his Anglican tradition.[59] It should be repeated here – if only in passing – that our generally favourable assessment of Bishop Robinson's ecclesiology is based upon what he has actually written about the Church and not what he has failed to say. It goes without saying that our basic disagreement is fundamental because the point at issue, namely the collegial nature and structure of the Church, is fundamental.[60]

We can, and have, agreed with him in his understanding of the Church as the Body of Christ and as the eschatological community, with certain reservations about the latter. He too, maintains that the Church has been founded and constituted by Christ upon the Prophets and the Apostles; that the Church is the one, holy, catholic, and apostolic community of those who acknowledge the Lordship

[56] *De Ecclesia*, II, 10.
[57] Cf. *ibid.*, III, 21.   [58] *Ibid.*, III, 18.
[59] For the most recent exposition of the teaching on the papacy, cf. *ibid.*, III, 22.
[60] 'The chief difficulty in the way of reunion lies in the two different concepts of the Church, and especially of the concrete organizational structure of the Church. . . . Ultimately, all questions about the concrete organizational structure of the Church are crystallized in the question of *ecclesiastical office* . . . [and] the heart of the matter of ecclesiastical office, the great stone of stumbling, is the Petrine office' (H. Küng, *The Council and Reunion*, pp. 188–189, 193). In his most recent book, *The New Reformation?*, Bishop Robinson writes: 'Nor do I mean that the issues on which we split are no longer real. In one sense nothing has changed. If challenged on the infallibility of the Pope or the assumption of the Virgin Mary I have not shifted my position, nor have the Romans moved from theirs' (p. 9).

of Christ; that this Resurrection Body of Christ is at once visible and invisible, animated by the Holy Spirit; that baptism incorporates one into this community and that the Eucharist is the centre of its life and the source of its unity. The harmony disappears abruptly, however, when we come to the question of ministry, and more specifically, the question of ecclesiastical office. And the heart of the matter of ecclesiastical office, the great stumbling-block for every Christian apart from the Catholic tradition, is the Petrine office. The question of the papacy is indeed the key question for the ecumenical movement. It has been said, in fact, that 'a negative answer to it seems often to be the one and only thing which unites Protestants of completely different denominations, and which to a great extent they will not even discuss'.[61] Bishop Robinson, as a matter of fact, does not discuss it at all in any of his writings on the Church and its ministry.[62]

THE NATURE AND PLACE OF THE CHURCH'S LITURGY

The Liturgy applies, of course, to the entire sacramental life of the Church, but for our purposes here we shall limit the discussion to the Eucharist.

Adhering to his own biblically-based High-Church ecclesiology, Robinson describes the Eucharist as the 'spring and pattern of all other Christian action',[63] 'the centre and power-house of everything . . . both within the life of the Christian congregation and in the

[61] H. Küng, *The Council and Reunion*, p. 193.

[62] The closest the bishop has come to such a discussion has been in a review of Oscar Cullmann's *Peter* for *The Church of England Newspaper* (September 7, 1953). In criticism of Cullmann's view, he writes: 'The "how" of apostolic succession may be in dispute, but not surely the fact that it must somehow reside in the "person" as well as the "word" of the Church, in the institution and not simply the canon.'

[63] *Liturgy Coming to Life*, p. 61; cf. also *In the End, God* . . ., p. 61; *On Being the Church in the World*, pp. 58 f. and 87: 'For the Eucharist is, *par excellence*, the pattern action of the Church, that by which the *Koinonia* is constituted and by which it is to be recognized, whether it be in a cathedral or in a prison-camp. One should not be able to come across the Community at any level without finding the Communion.'

world outside',[64] 'the heart of evangelism',[65] '*the* point where that
finished work (of Christ) is constantly renewed to the Church, as
those who have already been buried and raised with Christ in
Baptism come to share in the broken body and outpoured blood of
him whose crucified and life-giving body they are called to be'.[66]

The Eucharist must reflect the heart of the Gospel and the reality
of the Church. If the Eucharist is clericalized, then the Church and
the apostolate will appear to be clerical preserves. If it does not
meet the Pauline test (cf. I Cor. 14), it will make the Gospel appear
inplausible to the world.[67] The Eucharist is the supreme action of the
entire Body of Christ. The whole Church is the celebrant, over
which the bishop or priest presides.[68] The Church must feed upon
the Body of Christ in order that it may be created into the Body of
Christ:

> When St Paul introduced his remarks with the words, 'when you
> come together', he did not need to specify further that he was going on
> to speak of the Eucharist; for this was *the* thing, indeed the only thing,
> for which it was quite essential for the Church to 'come together'.
> This was the gathering for which the Lord's Day existed, and by
> which alone it was for hundreds of years distinguished from any other
> working day. To be a member of the Body and not to be *there* was *ipso
> facto* to be a sick member of the Body, whether physically or spiritually.
> Not to take one's place at the family table was necessarily to side
> with the world.[69]

The corporate character of the Eucharist does not consist simply
in the fact that the action is done together. It is not a question of
doing together what cannot be done alone, but rather by our
participation in the one bread (I Cor. 10.27) we become the one
Body of Christ. 'It is the Pauline mystery, so powerfully expounded

---

[64] *Liturgy Coming to Life*, p. 10.

[65] *Ibid.*, p. 11.   [66] *Ibid.*, p. 22.

[67] Cf. *On Being the Church in the World*, p. 69; cf. also 'The Tercentenary
of the Book of Common Prayer,' in *Parish and People*, no. 36, Epiphany, 1963,
pp. 15–19, where Bishop Robinson offers a critique of the Book of Common
Prayer on the basis of the four-fold criteria of St Paul: the liturgy must be
comprehensible, corporate, catholic, and must lead to conversion.

[68] Cf. *Liturgy Coming to Life*, p. 26; *On Being the Church in the World*, pp. 69,
79–80.

[69] *Liturgy Coming to Life*, p. 28.

by St Augustine, of the double sense of "the body" – that we *are* the body of Christ as we feed on the body of Christ . . . [and] with this goes the corollary that we cannot receive his body in the sacrament except as we are knit up into his body the Church: we cannot have Christ without his members. And the implications of that – that there *is* no Communion without community – are of unlimited consequence once we begin to take them seriously.'[70]

The Body of Christ is at the same time the eschatological community. At the Eucharist the 'powers of the age to come' are present: 'Week by week, in the Spirit (that "element of the end within the present"), on the Lord's day (itself the pledge of that "day of the Lord" when the rule of this world shall finally have passed to God and his Christ), the baptized come together to be built up into the body of Christ, into that part of the new resurrection order already at work within the structures of the old.'[71] And that is why the Eucharist cannot be considered a mere memorial service in which we remind ourselves of someone no longer with us. 'On the contrary, this is what brings the past *out* of the past – and the future *out* of the future – and makes them both operative in the here and now.'[72]

The Church is the pledge and instrument of the new creation. In the Eucharist the basic elements of the world are taken by Christ with all they represent of human life and over them are spoken the words of consecration. Outside the Eucharist the division between holy and common, secular and sacred, remains but within the Eucharist this division is abolished. 'I am interested in liturgy', Bishop Robinson states, 'only as the clue to the transfiguration of life by the Kingdom of God. And this I believe is the perspective of the New Testament.'[73]

The Eucharist, then, reflects the nature of the Church as the Body of Christ and as the eschatological community. The Eucharist points also to the mission of the Church in the world. 'The Communion is social dynamite, if we really take seriously the pattern of community

[70] *On Being the Church in the World*, p. 70; cf. *Liturgy Coming to Life*, p. 35.

[71] *On Being the Church in the World*, p. 61.

[72] *Idem, loc. cit.*; cf. also *Christ Comes In*, chapter IV, pp. 28 ff.; cf. also R. Schnackenburg, *Die Kirche im Neuen Testament*, I 6a; IV, 6 (pp. 39–40, 165–172).

[73] *Liturgy Coming to Life*, preface to the second edition (1963), p. xi; cf. also *The New Reformation?*, pp. 82–88.

known at the altar. The Church discovered that, in time, in the case of slavery. We have to discover it in terms of race and class and all that is involved for the distribution of the world's resources in the practice, in which we indulge so thoughtlessly each Sunday, *of the absolutely unconditional sharing of bread.*[74] 'Liturgy coming to life' (the title of Bishop Robinson's book) is not simply liturgical renewal for its own sake or even for the sake of the Church. Rather it is a question of liturgy coming uncomfortably close to life. 'For liturgy is nothing less than the Gospel of the Word made flesh in action, Christ through his body about his saving work, taking the things of this world and, through the power of his sacrifice, leaving *none* of them untouched.'[75]

An apt summary-expression of this relationship between the liturgy and the Church's mission to the world (social action) is contained in his recent book, *Honest to God:*

> The test of worship is how far it makes us *more sensitive* to 'the beyond in our midst', to the Christ in the hungry, the naked, the homeless and the prisoner. Only if we are *more likely* to recognize him there after attending an act of worship is that worship Christian rather than a piece of religiosity in Christian dress. That is what is implied in Jesus' saying that 'the sabbath was made for man, not man for the sabbath'. The whole of our religious observance and church-going must be prepared to submit to its test.[76]

There are broad lines of agreement between the preceding views

[74] *Liturgy Coming to Life,* p. 37; cf. also *On Being the Church in the World,* pp. 61–62, 67–69; *Christ Comes In,* pp. 30–31.

[75] *Liturgy Coming to Life,* pp. 43–44; cf. especially *On Being the Church in the World,* p. 71: 'Just as this Eucharistic action is the pattern of all Christian action, the sharing of this Bread the sign for the sharing of all bread, so this Fellowship is the germ of all society renewed in Christ. . . . The destiny which Christ holds out for matter, for power and for society, is comprehended in the single great purpose, already begun, of the conforming of the body of our humiliation – this entire structure of sorrow, sin and death – to the likeness of his glorious body. That is the Christian's goal, and his social task. And the point *par excellence* where the new creation breaks through into this, where the pattern and the power of the new world is given, and where the new community which is its instrument is fashioned, is the Holy Communion. Let us then never lose grip on its centrality, nor allow ourselves to reckon liturgy of little significance, if these great social concerns are at the heart of what we mean by the Gospel.'

[76] p. 90.

of Bishop Robinson and the Catholic doctrine expounded by the Second Vatican Council in its constitution *De Sacra Liturgia*. The bishop's liturgical perspective would diverge from Catholic teaching in so far as it would incorporate and be based upon those areas of his ecclesiology to which we have already taken exception; namely, his fundamental position on the collegial nature and structure of the Church.[77]

These significant areas of disagreement notwithstanding, the lines of agreement are genuinely broad indeed. The liturgy, and specifically the Eucharist, *is* 'the outstanding means whereby the faithful may express in their lives, and manifest to others, the mystery of Christ and the real nature of the true Church'.[78] And this has always been so since the time of the Apostles and the primitive Christian community (cf. Acts 2.42).[79] The Church truly participates in the priesthood of Christ, for the liturgy is an exercise of the priestly office of Jesus Christ and he always associates his whole Body with himself in the worship of the Father.[80] For the Christian people is a royal priesthood by reason of baptism;[81] consequently, liturgical services are always celebrations of the whole Church and pertain to the whole body of the Church.[82] The liturgy, then, is the 'summit towards which the action of the Church tends and likewise the source from which all her power flows'.[83] The liturgy of the Church stands as the pivotal point of the Christian life, reflecting the nature of the Church and providing the impetus and the challenge for her mission in the world.

SUMMARY: PART ONE

For Bishop John A. T. Robinson the Church is both the Body of Christ and the eschatological community, and both realities are united in the notion of the Resurrection Body. For this Body of

[77] It is beyond the scope of this study to examine specific areas of Robinson's sacramental theology. The bishop admits, for example, that the Mass can be called a sacrifice but he does not choose to develop this point. Cf. *On Being the Church in the World*, p. 78.

[78] *De Sacra Liturgia*, intro., para 2.

[79] Cf. *ibid.*, I, 6.

[80] *Ibid.*, I, 7.

[81] *Ibid.*, I, 14.

[82] *Ibid.*, I, 26.

[83] *Ibid.*, I, 10.

Christ is a community-in-history and a community-in-the-Spirit. It bears an essential relationship to the Kingdom of God, for it is 'always and only' the instrument of the *Kingdom* and, as such, is subordinate to the Kingdom as the ministry is subordinate to the Church. As the Son of Man himself existed as a 'sign' to 'this generation' (cf. Luke 11.30), a sign of the Kingdom, of what God was doing in its midst, so too the primary task of the Church is 'to produce not settlements, but "signs" . . . [it] exists to be the sign, the first-fruits, of the New Humanity'.[84] The ministry is a function of this mission and the liturgy is its 'summit and source'. It is in this light that we should understand his most recent definition of the Church in *The New Reformation?*: 'It is indeed the dedicated nucleus of those who actively acknowledge Jesus as Lord and have committed themselves to membership and mission within the visible sacramental fellowship of the Spirit.'[85]

The major difficulty with this doctrine of the Church is that the Church in her very nature and essential structure is collegial in character and her unity is made permanent and visible in the Petrine office. And while the priesthood of Christ has been committed truly to the Church as a Body, nevertheless there *is* a difference of *essence* as well as degree between the priesthood of the People of God in general, on the one hand, and that of the apostolic college and their ordained associates, on the other.

It is within this particular context and with these qualifications that we begin our investigation of Bishop Robinson's most recent works, *Honest to God* and *The New Reformation?*, in which the question of the Church's *mission* rather than her *nature* is paramount.

[84] *The New Reformation?*, pp. 103–104.
[85] *Ibid.*, p. 48.   [86] *De Ecclesia*, II, 9.

Part Two

THE MISSION OF THE CHURCH

5

THE CHURCH:
THE SECULAR COMMUNITY

IN a world that has become, or has become again, purely "worldly",' Yves Congar has written, 'the Church finds herself forced, if she would still be anything at all, to be simply the Church, witness to the Gospel and the Kingdom of God, through Jesus Christ and in view of him. That is what men need, that is what they expect of her. In fact if we listed all their most valid claims on the Church we should find that they amounted to this: that she be less *of* the world and more *in* the world; that she be simply the Church of Jesus Christ, the conscience of men in the light of the Gospel, but that she be this with her whole heart.'[1]

In this view the mission of the Church is constituted by her relation to the Kingdom and to the world. She is the witness and instrument of the Kingdom, and the servant of the world. This is Bishop Robinson's position, as it is Congar's. For John A. T. Robinson an accurate ecclesiology depends upon the establishment of a proper relationship between Church and Kingdom of God, and this relationship must entail, in its very essence, a subordination of the former to the latter. The Church is the instrument of the Kingdom. She is, at one and the same time, Body of Christ and eschatological community, 'the dedicated nucleus of those who actively acknowledge Jesus as Lord and have committed themselves to membership and mission within the visible sacramental fellowship of the Spirit'.[2]

[1] *Power and Poverty in the Church* (tr. D. Attwater), London: Geoffrey Chapman, 1964, p. 137.
[2] *The New Reformation?*, p. 48.

Yet this is not to be considered its *normal* form of existence, when it is distinctively being itself. The Church is not something gathered together in one place so much as a reality 'embedded as seeds of light within the dark world'.[3] The house of God is not the Church but the world, wherein the Church dwells and labours as its servant.[4] The Church must be the incarnation, however imperfect, of the Son of Man on earth, 'for men today cannot see Jesus as the Son of God until they have seen him as the Son of Man'[5] – *incognito*, in the 'gracious neighbour', in the Servant Church.[6]

This is, in very abbreviated form, the basic perspective of Bishop Robinson with regard to the mission of the Church. In this chapter we shall examine more fully this second major area of his doctrine of the Church. The opening quotation from Yves Congar should indicate clearly enough that Robinson is not alone in his basic insight. Accordingly, we shall also examine the sources from which he has drawn, as well as those other theological works which he may have chosen to ignore or, more likely, which simply did not come to his attention. We shall limit ourseves primarily to the notion of the Church as Servant in the world, i.e. as the *secular community*, leaving for the sixth chapter the question of the Church's mission to preach the gospel to all mankind, i.e. the Church as the *missionary community*.

THE CHURCH AS SECULAR COMMUNITY ACCORDING TO BISHOP ROBINSON

The Church is not simply a humanitarian social agency which exists to serve the material and psychological needs of the world. The Church is a secular community in the sense that it exists *in* the world and *for* the world, but ultimately all is for the sake of the Kingdom[7] – that the reign of God in Christ might extend to, and be

---

[3] *The New Reformation?*, p. 48.
[4] *Ibid.*, cf. p. 92.   [5] *Ibid.*, p. 40.   [6] *Ibid.*, cf. pp. 32–38.
[7] Cf. 'The Ministry and the Laity', p. 21; 'For ultimately the Christian is neither church-centred nor world-centred, but Kingdom-centred. For the Church is the instrument of God for reducing the world to the Kingdom and the ministry of the laity is the ministry of God *both* within the structures of the Church *and* within the structures of the world'; cf. also *Honest to God*, p. 140: 'The true radical is the man who continually subjects the Church to the judgement of the

acknowledged by, all creation (cf. Eph. 1.9–10, 22–23; Col. 1.13–20).[8] Indeed, 'the whole existence of the Church', Robinson insists, 'is orientated towards that area of life which, within this age, does *not yet* acknowledge the sovereignty of God established over it in Christ. The stress on the boundaries of this age, or *saeculum*, will explain also why . . . it is impossible to be concerned with the witness of the Church in the "secular" world without constantly becoming involved in the issues of eschatology.'[9]

Therefore, there is an essential and intimate connection between the Church as the eschatological community and the Church as the secular community. As the eschatological community the Church is, as we have seen in the third chapter, a community-in-history and in-the-Spirit. The Church is the place where, *de facto*, the universal Lordship of Christ is recognized and acknowledged, where this Kingship of the Lord is embodied, or at least should be embodied, more fully than in any other section of humanity. For the Church exists as 'a kind of firstfruits' of God's redemptive purpose (cf. James 1.18) and as the instrument by which the rest of creation is to be restored and conformed to the image of his Son.

But to say that the Church is the instrument of the Kingdom and the servant of God in the world is not to assert that the Church is the only agent of God in this world. It is the perennial temptation of the Church to believe this, 'to assume that what God is doing in this world he must be doing through the Church, that the space to watch, as it were, if one really wants to see what God is up to, is the Church papers'.[10] Certainly no non-Christian would ever imagine this, nor is it a concept that is to be derived from the Bible. The People of God in the Old Testament could not be described as the rudder by which the course of history is steered. It is more like a cork bobbing in the ocean borne this way and that, and at times almost completely submerged, by the events and currents of history. And

---

Kingdom, to the claims of God in the increasingly non-religious world which the Church exists to serve'; cf. also 'Kingdom, Church and Ministry', *passim*, and *The World that God Loves*, pp. 4, 6.

[8] Cf. *The Body: A Study in Pauline Theology*, pp. 71, 82–83; and 'Ascendancy', pp. 8–9.

[9] *On Being the Church in the World*, pp. 7–8.

[10] *Ibid.*, p. 20.

yet the history of this People provided the clue to the understanding, and even more to the redemption, of this process. 'But the answer to the question "What is God doing?" is at any moment just as likely to be given in the operations of Pharaoh, or the King of Assyria, or Cyrus King of Persia, as in any activity which today would be regarded as the work of the Church.'[11] And the same holds true for the New Testament, especially in the Apocalypse, the only New Testament book, according to Robinson, which deals specifically with the theology of the secular world and of secular power. The Church alone holds the clue to God's redemptive purpose (Eph. 3.10) and is the instrument of his reconciling work (Col. 1.18–20), but 'it is nowhere claimed in the Bible as the mainspring of God's action in history. The Christian society must always be expecting God to be acting decisively outside its ranks.'[12] Thus, the Church is truly a community-in-history, the salt of the earth and the leaven in the lump of creation, redeeming the world from the powers of this present age and giving witness to the Lordship of Christ. But this is to be understood with the reservations presented above, and it is in this context, and with these qualifications, that the notion of the Servant Church and the secular community must be evaluated.

The Church is also a community-in-the-Spirit, that is to say that the Servant Church is in common possession of the Holy Spirit.[13] The life of the Church is essentially a response, a hearkening unto obedience of the Spirit. The prerequisite of all reformation and of all ministry, if it is to be fruitful and faithful to the gospel, is sensitivity to what the Spirit is saying to the Church and to the world. Our day, Robinson feels, is marked by a consciousness of the ground moving under one's feet. 'There has been a troubling of the waters (cf. John 5.1–9) such as betokens the quickening power of the Spirit, a rustling in the tree-tops such as David was given as a sign that the Lord had passed on before him and that he must act (II Sam. 5.24).'[14] A deeper awareness of the Church's mission in the world must be developed if the quickening power of the Spirit is to be efficacious.

---

[11] *On Being the Church in the World*, pp. 20–21.
[12] *Ibid.*, p. 21.   [13] Cf. Chapter 3, pp. 62 ff., above.
[14] *The New Reformation?*, p. 17.

The Church must see herself, in other words, as 'the world's deacon',[15] as the Servant of God and the Son of Man in the world. This self-awareness will not be able to develop if, paradoxically, those areas of Church-renewal – the biblical, liturgical and ecumenical movements – succeed only in strengthening the Church *against* the world rather than in releasing the Church *for* the world.[16] She must exercise a leavening influence in the body of this world, serving within, rather than merely alongside, the structures of the world.[17] The Church must take seriously the incarnational and sacramental principles, which is to say that she must take seriously the body of history.[18] The Christian promise is of a 'renovated cosmos which will include a new heaven and a new earth, an order, that is to say, in which all things, spiritual *and* material, shall be fully reconciled in Christ. It is a hope for history, not a release from history.'[19] The partition between the sacred and the profane must be dissolved at many points, and especially at the central point, the Eucharist. 'Liturgy is essentially and primarily a secular activity, as the origin of the word in the sphere of public works testifies. It is concerned with matter, with society, with action – *ordinary* matter, society and action – *at the level of the holy*, at the level at which it is touched and recreated by the transforming Spirit of Christ. It is not concerned with a special world of its own, but with the making sacred of the secular.'[20] Christ must be met at the centre of life, even in those areas *'where a religious sector can no longer be presupposed as a special point of entry or contact'*.[21]

It is within this theological and historical framework that Robinson constructs his theology of the Servant Church. He develops his argument in the following way (and we are – necessarily – anticipating certain questions that will be raised and discussed in the next chapter): To larger and larger numbers of our generation the

---

[15] *The World that God Loves*, p. 6.

[16] *The New Reformation?*, p. 25.

[17] *Ibid.*, p. 27.

[18] *On Being the Church in the World*, p. 34; cf. also pp 14 ff., where he insists upon the continuity between this age and the age to come.

[19] 'The Christian Hope', in *Christian Faith and Communist Faith* (1953), p. 214.

[20] *Liturgy Coming to Life*, p. xi.

[21] *The Honest to God Debate*, p. 271.

Christian gospel, in the manner and form in which it is preached, is
no longer the good news, and the Church, to the extent that she is
identified with the function of preaching the Word and duly admin-
istering the sacraments, has become progressively more irrelevant.
The world of today is *not* asking the question of the Reformers, 'How
can I find a gracious God?' It *is* asking, 'How can I find a gracious
neighbour?' And its starting-point is not the Church but mankind
itself. It begins not from revelation, in which it has no prior confi-
dence, but from relationships, which it is prepared to treat with a
greater seriousness than any generation before it. And it proceeds
inductively, from the evidence of experience, rather than deduc-
tively, from the certainties of authority. The question with which we
are presented is this: 'How *in this situation* is the Gospel of Christ to
be preached and what is the place of the Church? Is it possible for
Christians to accept this shift in the entire frame of reference – and
not to sell out? This, I believe, is a very big question, the biggest
question for the future of Christianity in our day. I should be foolish
if I returned a confident or a simple answer.'[22]

The theology which is demanded by this totally new situation is a
theology that must start from Christ as the way to the Father. The
central text of the old Reformation was the *sola fide* of Luther; for the
new Reformation it will be John 14.9: 'He who has seen me has seen
the Father.' But we cannot stop there, for this generation asks the
further question: 'But, Lord, when did we see you?' (Matt. 25.37–39,
44). And the answer to that question is given in the parable of the
Sheep and the Goats (Matt. 25.32–33),[23] in terms of the Son of Man
incognito, that is to say, in terms of the 'gracious neighbour'. This is a
generation in which it might be said that Christ is no longer expected.
The situation is similar to those on the road to Emmaus who look
back, some with genuine regret, at the Jesus of history as the one who
might have been the Christ. And yet on the road to Emmaus Jesus did
not, and does not, confront us as the Christ, but simply as the stranger
who comes alongside in our questioning and our sadness. 'It is only
from there, as the man for others and with others, that he can make

[22] *The New Reformation?*, p. 34.
[23] Cf. Robinson's own study of this parable in *Twelve New Testament Studies*,
pp 76–93.

himself known to them as the Messiah of whom their Scriptures spoke.'[24] This story, the parable of the Sheep and the Goats and the story of Jesus' final appearance to his disciples by the lakeside in John 21 have a peculiarly compelling power for our generation, 'for they all tell of one who comes unknown and uninvited into the human situation, disclosing himself as the gracious neighbour before he can be recognized as Master and Lord'.[25] With these passages Robinson would link the story of the foot-washing in John 13,[26] 'where, even to those who call him Lord and Master, he can make known the meaning of that lordship only by becoming the servant of all. . . . It is indeed central to the Christian revelation for any age. For the very meaning of the Incarnation is that the divine enters through the stable door of ordinary human history and everyday experience.'[27] Bishop Robinson proceeds to suggest that the primary task of theology and of the Church in our time could be described as making such a meeting possible again. 'For the effect of the Church's work has been to strip the Christ of his incognito. It has placarded him to men as the Son of God without allowing them to meet him as the Son of Man.'[28]

The task of the Church, which is the Body of Christ, is 'to *be* this Son of Man on earth, allowing its imperfect incarnation to be judged constantly by *the* Incarnation'.[29] And so the Church must be an open society, 'the accepting community' whose chief characteristic is that it is prepared to meet men where they are and accept them for what they are.[30] For mankind will ultimately be judged by its own humanity, by what it really means to be a man, and 'it will understand that truth and accept it only as it *actually finds itself convicted by the Son of man on earth*, that is, by the Church as she takes a towel and girds herself, by her ministers and her members as they "do judgement" for the least of his brethren'.[31] And yet this is *not* the image which the Church has uniformly projected: 'The whole

[24] *The New Reformation?*, p. 36.   [25] *Idem, loc. cit.*

[26] Cf. Robinson's specific study of this incident: 'The Significance of the Foot-Washing', in *Neotestamentica et Patristica*, Leiden: Brill, 1962, pp. 144–147.

[27] *The New Reformation?*, p. 36.

[28] *Ibid.*, p. 37.

[29] *Ibid.*, p. 42, n. 1.   [30] *Ibid.*, p. 46.

[31] *On Being the Church in the World*, p. 145.

tendency of the Reformation-Counter-reformation era was to think of the Church in terms of the gathered or the excommunicating group. It *defined* the Church when it was *out* of the world, as the salt piled, clean and white, in the cellar, as the leaven unmixed with the meal. And this is precisely when it is *not* being itself or performing its essential function. For it is distinctively itself when it cannot be seen and tasted for itself at all, but when it is transforming whatever it is in.'[32]

The Church, then, is not simply a circle of light bounded on all sides by darkness, a community of the elect – as the Reformers would have it – gathered apart from and over against the world. And the last thing the Church exists to be is 'an organization for the religious'[33] whose main function is 'to make or keep man religious'.[24] On the contrary, 'its charter is to be the servant of the world'.[35] In contrast with the 'unhappy distinction' between the visible and invisible Church proposed by the Reformers, the distinction for our time must be that of the 'manifest' and the 'latent' Church, corresponding to the distinction between the Christ 'acknowledged' and the Christ 'incognito'. 'And "where Christ is" – *where either Christ is* – "there is the Church".'[36]

In the light of this new theology of the Church, our concept of her mission must be re-examined and re-evaluated. The Church is not simply a circle of light into which as many people must be drawn as possible. Their distance from Christ cannot be identified simply with their distance from the manifest Church. 'Indeed, it is religious presumption to assume that Christ is in the centre of the Church's circle and not in the dark world. Moreover, the question insistently

---

[32] *The New Reformation?*, pp. 46–47.
[33] *Honest to God*, p. 134.　　　　[34] *Ibid.*, p. 139.　　　　[35] *Ibid.*, p. 134.
[36] *The New Reformation?*, p. 47; cf. also 'The Ministry and the Laity', pp. 21–22, where Robinson is critical of Hendrik Kraemer's *A Theology of the Laity* (London: Lutterworth Press, 1958). According to Robinson, Kraemer stresses the ministry *of* the Church *to* the world. 'But the New Testament speaks of a ministry of God which is not "of" the Church, and which need not, therefore, be exercised by committed Christians. It would be truer to say that some are called to the ministry of the Kingdom (or perhaps better the ministry of the King) through the structures of the Church, and some are called to the ministry of the Kingdom through the structures of the world. It is these latter who seem to me most in need of the help of the Church (whether they are Christians or not) – and who least get it.'

posed by the Gospels is not how far men are from the manifest Church but how far they are from the kingdom of God.'[37] The enlargement of the circle of light is not the primary mission of the Church, for this cannot be substantiated by the witness of the New Testament. While the New Testament *does* point toward the consummation of all things *in Christ*, it never suggests that all men will be *in the Church*, not within the present age at any rate. In fact, from beginning to end the Bible consistently visualizes the covenant people as a minority instrument of the Kingdom, whose minority status is not a scandal.

The mission of the manifest Church must be directed towards the Kingdom rather than towards itself. The Church must make it possible for men and women to be met by Christ *where they are*, that is, within the context and thought-forms of the latent church. It must preach the Gospel to the poor, and, if necessary, in the entirely non-religious terms announced by Jesus, i.e. of the release of prisoners and the recovery of sight for the blind (cf. Luke 4.18) – even if they never say, 'Lord, Lord!' The Church, then, must curb its instinctive urge to remove rather than respect 'the incognitos under which the parable of the Sheep and the Goats alone shows it possible for the Christ to meet and to judge the mass of men. And the incognitos of that parable are those of *humanity* and *secularity*: the Son of Man wills to be met in an utterly disinterested concern for persons for their own sake, and in relationships that have nothing distinctively religious about them.'[38]

In summary: If the gospel is to become for men again the *good news*, they must be able to discover the gracious neighbour in the accepting community, whether latent or manifest. Christ must be allowed to confront them as the Son of Man through a Church which must be the Servant of God in the world. As a consequence the Church must become genuinely and increasingly *lay*, not in the sense of abolishing its sacramental ministers but rather in the sense that the laity is the *laos* or people of God *in the world*, for whom the things of this world have a meaning and value in themselves and not simply in terms of some higher reference.[39]

[37] *The New Reformation?*, p. 48.   [38] *Ibid.*, p. 50.
[39] Cf. *Honest to God*, p. 137; cf. also 'The Ministry and the Laity', p. 18.

One final issue remains to be discussed; namely, the implications of the theology of the Servant Church for its structural reform, What is alluded to in *Honest to God* is developed more fully in *The New Reformation?* In the former book the bishop was concerned only that the Church not become merely an organization for the religious, whose main function is to make or keep men religious, but rather that it embody the life of 'the man for others' – 'the love whereby we are brought completely into one with the Ground of our being, manifesting itself in the unreconciled relationships of our existence'.[40] At first glance, *Honest to God* maintains very little interest in the structural aspect of the Church, suggesting perhaps an amorphous community morally united by means of a common outlook and perspective. This simply emphasizes a fundamental point to which we shall return in our final summary and critique; namely, that the ecclesiology of Bishop John A. T. Robinson cannot be culled from the best-selling *Honest to God* and that attempts to do so will lead inevitably to misinterpretation and misunderstanding. *The New Reformation?*, on the other hand, offers a more adequate ecclesiological landscape and it was written precisely to continue where *Honest to God* left off, attempting to answer the question: 'So what for the Church?' 'Can these bones live?' (Ezek. 37.3), he asks. 'Can it possibly be the carrier of the new life for the new age?'[41] There are many in our generation, he observes, who would answer these questions in the negative, who would disavow any further interest in the reformation of the Church. Robinson personally dissents from their view for he knows 'in his bones that he could not put himself outside, [but he wants] to plead for those who feel that they must'.[42]

But for him the tension cannot be broken so easily. The Christian cannot simply renounce the question of what the Church must do to revitalize itself. 'I believe in fact,' he writes, 'that re-formation is a category we must use, and my continued exploration of what a new Reformation might mean is testimony to this ineluctable conviction. Until it is finally proved otherwise, the Christian must believe that the Church – and he himself as a member of it – can be used rather

---

[40] *Honest to God*, p. 82; cf. also pp. 134, 139.
[41] *The New Reformation?*, p. 13.
[42] *Ibid.*, p. 15.

than discarded: "Be it unto me according to thy word".[43] And yet, by the same token, he cannot command renewal. The history of the Church is marked by premature attempts at reform, and none were successful until they coincided with 'the moment, and the movement, of the Spirit'.[44] For all reformation is essentially a response to a motion of the Holy Spirit.

In the old Reformation of Protestantism there were produced new confessions of faith, liturgies, forms of church order, denominations, and so forth. It was an age of affirmation and theological reconstruction. But in our time, in this era of the new Reformation, this current response to the Spirit – if it be such – will be distinguished from the earlier one by the fact that it is 'a time of reticence, of stripping down, of travelling light. The Church will go through its baggage and discover how much it can better do without, alike in doctrine and in organization.'[45] In the old Reformation 'a cluster of little catholicisms was born, each reproducing the characteristics of the parent, with its own ministry and sacraments, its own buildings and budgets'.[46] Today, on the other hand, the Church must come to grips with the fact that it is heavily institutionalized, with a crushing investment in maintenance; that it has 'the characteristics of the dinosaur and the battleship'.[47] The image is one of a Church 'remarkably well protected for its mission of being the servant of the world'.[48] There is no easy answer to this problem, of course, but at least the guiding principles ought to be clear: that only from the Cross can the resurrection of the Church begin, that the Church, if she is to be truly the Son of Man on earth, must be willing to surrender her worldly security and so dramatize for all mankind what it really means to exist for others.[49] The Church must exist within and not merely alongside the structures and institutions of society. The movement of re-formation will come by the Church 'allowing *the forms* of her renewed life to grow around *the shapes of worldly need*', but the ecclesiological development in accordance with this pattern and need must proceed with care lest this instrument of service be not only of the wrong shape but also of the wrong size. It must respect

[43] *The New Reformation?*, p. 16.
[44] *Idem, loc. cit.*   [45] *Ibid.*, p. 20.   [46] *Ibid.*, p. 25.
[47] *Ibid.*, p. 26.   [48] *Idem, loc. cit.*   [49] *Ibid.*, p. 31.

the principles of congregationalism and of the 'house-Church', on the one hand, and yet not make these the principle of justification. There are needs which transcend the resources and aims of the local community and which call for the witness and service of the Church on a world-wide scale.

Can the Church survive this structural upheaval? Can the Church really be there in the midst of all the ambiguities of the 'secular hope'? Is the Church *free* enough to be there, to let itself 'take shape around his servant presence in the world'? Robinson's faith is that the Church can do all of these things – 'just'. 'And that is why', he concludes, 'I believe in a new Reformation as a real and exciting divine possibility.'[50]

AN EVALUATION OF THE SOURCES OF ROBINSON'S THEOLOGY OF THE SERVANT CHURCH

The Church as the secular community has a relationship both to the Kingdom of God and to the world. The latter relationship is, of course, the distinctive one, but it is poorly understood if a proper eschatological perspective is lacking. These points have been discussed already in the preceding pages, and particularly in the third chapter of this study. Our interest in this section of the present chapter is to trace and identify the various sources from which Bishop Robinson has drawn in developing his concept of the Church's mission in the world.

'The true radical', he writes in *Honest to God*, 'is the man who continually subjects the Church to the judgement of the Kingdom, to the claims of God in the increasingly non-religious world which the Church exists to serve.'[51] It cannot be repeated too often that the bishop's insistence on a right relationship between the Church and the Kingdom is fundamental and central to his entire ecclesiology. The Church is the instrument of the Kingdom, and as such is subordinate to it.

The roots of this particular area of his doctrine of the Servant Church can be traced, as we have already suggested in the third

[50] *The New Reformation*, p. 99.
[51] P. 140; cf. also 'Kingdom, Church and Ministry', *passim*.

chapter, to the influence of Oscar Cullmann, and particularly his essay, 'The Kingship of Christ and the Church in the New Testament'.[52] Herein the Church is presented as the instrument of the Kingdom of God, located always between the Kingdom accomplished and the Kingdom acknowledged. Its entire existence is orientated towards that area of life where the universal kingship of God in Christ is not yet accepted. Thus, the Church lives under the judgement of the day when Church and Kingdom will be identical and the temple will be no more, but in the meantime (in the 'between-the-times') it exists for the sake of life in this age (or *saeculum*) in which Christ is King but not yet crowned. For Cullmann the essential mark of the Church is its acknowledgement of the Lordship of Christ and its primary task is to preach the Gospel to all mankind: 'No failure need discourage the Church in its work, since the greatest earthly failure that ever was is at the very centre of the faith of the New Testament: the cross of Christ, which, to the Christian, means victory over all hostile powers and the eschatological beginning of the present kingship of Christ, which can only be superseded by the Kingdom of God.'[53] Cullmann does not develop the notion of the Church's mission beyond the task of preaching the gospel. The idea of the Servant Church does not occupy his attention. Cullmann, then, can be regarded as an important, but by no means the most important, source of Bishop Robinson's theology of the Church as the secular community. But in the over-all view of the bishop's ecclesiology one cannot afford to underestimate Cullmann's inspiration, particularly in impressing Robinson with the subordinate relationship between Church and Kingdom.

A second major source of Bishop Robinson's theology of the Servant Church is Paul Tillich. But whereas Cullmann influenced Robinson very early in his academic career as some of his initial writings testify,[54] Tillich appears relatively late. Robinson had read Tillich

---

[52] Reprinted in *The Early Church* (1956), pp. 105–137; cf. Chapter 3, pp. 49–51, where I have summarized Cullmann's thought at greater length.

[53] *The Early Church*, p. 134; R. Schnackenburg's criticisms of Cullmann's position should be recalled: cf. *God's Rule and Kingdom*, pp. 296 ff. and 343 ff.; cf. also Cullmann's 'Eschatology and Missions in the New Testament' in the Dodd *Festschrift*, pp. 412–413, and *Christ and Time*, pp. 157 ff.

[54] For example, *The Body* (1952) and 'The One Baptism' (1953).

and had used his *Systematic Theology* in conjunction with various doctrinal courses which were assigned him and even went so far as to read one of Tillich's sermons at Wells Theological College in place of an address of his own. Yet Tillich was not particularly relevant to Robinson's work as a biblical theologian and exegete during the Cambridge period. Tillich himself had admitted to a certain scepticism regarding the historicity of the Fourth Gospel, the object of primary interest for John A. T. Robinson.[55]

Tillich came into theological focus during Robinson's famous illness at which time *Honest to God* was conceived. But the use of Tillich in that book is directed almost exclusively to the content and presentation of the Christian message and not to the community which is commissioned to preserve and preach that message. It is not until his most recent book, *The New Reformation?*, that Robinson employs Tillich for his doctrine of the Church, and it is not the three-volume *Systematic Theology* that provides the material but rather a series of unpublished propositions quoted in an early study of Tillich in 1952.[56] Herein is contained the basic distinction between the *manifest* and the *latent* Church: the former is the definite historical community which acknowledges the Lordship of Christ and in which the New Being is actualized directly and 'manifestly'; the latter is an indefinite historical group which actualizes the New Being within paganism, Judaism, or humanism. Where Christ is (the Christ acknowledged or the Christ *incognito*), there is the Church. As seems to have been the case in *Honest to God*, Robinson accepts the terminology and, to an extent, the ideas of Tillich, but then employs them to his own use, often at variance with Tillich's purpose. Thus, Robinson draws a number of implications from the *manifest – latent* distinction for his theology of the Church's mission (as we indicated earlier in the chapter) and merely notes – without specifically endorsing – Tillich's position concerning the marks of the Church. Tillich treats them as the marks of the Spiritual Community, latent *or* manifest. They are neither unambiguous in the historic churches,

[55] Cf. J. A. T. Robinson, 'The Place of the Fourth Gospel', in *The Roads Converge* (ed. P. Gardner-Smith), London: Arnold, 1963, pp. 53–54.

[56] Cf. *The Theology of Paul Tillich* (ed. C. W. Kegley and R. W. Bretall), New York: Macmillan, 1952, p. 259, wherein Tillich's unpublished *Propositions* (Part IV, p. 27) are presented.

nor absent outside them.[57] Tillich's ecclesiology is open to far more criticism certainly than Robinson's, but it cannot be the concern of this study. It is sufficient to note the origin and significance of the distinction between the latent and the manifest Church and to endorse the limited use which the bishop makes of it.

The third major theological source is also the most important one: Dietrich Bonhoeffer. Under the impact of his writings, and especially the last fifty pages of the famous *Letters and Papers from Prison*,[58] Robinson's ecclesiological thought and writings have been directed almost exclusively to the question of the relevance of the Church in the modern industrialized, urbanized society, that is to say, with the mission rather than with the nature of the Church. It is from Bonhoeffer that Robinson derives the main inspiration for his idea of the Servant Church as well as the basic framework of the supporting argumentation; namely, the notion of Christ as 'the man for others'. 'The Church is her true self', Bonhoeffer wrote just before his death at the hands of the Nazis, 'only when she exists for humanity. . . . She must take her part in the social life of the world, not lording it over men, but helping and serving them. She must tell men, whatever their calling, what it means to live in Christ, to exist for others.'[59] Other views of Bonhoeffer have a very familiar ring in the light of our study of Bishop Robinson's position in the first part of this chapter: 'To be a Christian', Bonhoeffer wrote, 'does not mean to be religious in a particular way, to cultivate some particular form of asceticism (as a sinner, a penitent, or a saint), but to be a man. It is not some religious act which makes Christ what he is, but participation in the suffering of God in the life of the world.'[60] 'What is Christianity, and indeed what *is* Christ for us today? . . . We are proceeding towards a time of no religion at all. . . . How can Christ become the Lord even of those with no religion? If religion is not more than the garment of Christianity . . . then what is a religionless Christianity?'[61] 'The Christian, unlike the devotees of

[57] Tillich continues to employ these concepts in his *Systematic Theology*, vol. III, London: Nisbet, 1965, pp. 152–157, but he now prefers to speak of the difference between 'the Spiritual Community in its latency and in its manifestation'.

[58] London: SCM Press, 1953, and London: Collins, 1959. The following notes will refer to the Collins edition.

[59] *Ibid.*, p. 166.   [60] *Ibid.*, p. 123.   [61] *Ibid.*, p. 91.

the salvation myths, does not need a last refuge in the eternal from earthly tasks and difficulties. But like Christ himself ("My God, my God, why has thou forsaken me?") he must drink the earthly cup to the lees, and only in his doing that is the crucified and risen Lord with him, and he crucified and risen with Christ.'[62]

As Bonhoeffer viewed the world in 1945 he saw the 'coming of age' of humanity, the decay of religion in this new 'world come of age', and specifically the decline of the Protestant Church. 'The decisive factor: the Church on the defensive. Unwillingness to take risks in the service of humanity.'[63] The encounter with God, if it is to be genuine, must be through an encounter with Christ, 'the man for others'. For in Jesus we see one whose only concern is for others. 'This freedom from self, maintained to the point of death, [is] the sole ground of his omnipotence, omniscience, and ubiquity. Faith is [the] participation in this Being of Jesus (incarnation, cross, and resurrection) . . . God in human form . . . [as] man existing for others, and hence the Crucified.'[64] The consequence of all of this for the Church is that she is her true self only when she exists for humanity, when she willingly accepts the role of the Son of Man on earth and the Servant of God in the world.

In the light of the preceding it is hardly surprising that Robinson should have described Dietrich Bonhoeffer as 'the John the Baptist of the new Reformation'[65] and said that his contribution is 'probably the most radically original of all those I quoted (including Tillich and Bultmann) and could not have been made before the middle of the twentieth century'.[66] 'People were not slow in realizing', the bishop has remarked, 'that here indeed were ideas to split rocks, that to speak as he does of man "come of age" as being "radically without religion" would have wide implications for the future course of Christianity.'[67] Honest to God and The New Reformation? are both notable attempts to develop those implications.

Robinson incorporates much of Bonhoeffer's vision into his own doctrine of the Church. This is evident beyond any doubt. And for

[62] Letters and Papers from Prison, p. 112.
[63] Ibid., p. 164. [64] Ibid., pp. 164–165.
[65] The New Reformation?, p. 23.
[66] The Honest to God Debate, p. 272.
[67] Keeping in Touch with Theology (pamphlet), 1963, p. 4.

the most part he has used him judiciously, conscious of the fact that Bonhoeffer by himself and pushed to extremes 'can be very dangerous in quite a lot of things'.[68] His ecclesiology, naturally enough, is decidedly Lutheran but with some Barthian elements. The Church can be called the 'locus and embodiment of revelation' and yet it is only a personal community and in no sense a hierarchical institution. It is a community called into existence by, and continually dependent upon, the preached Word. As a personal community the Church is the unity of act and being. It is act in that it exists only by virtue of the act of faith. This faith, however, is not only the Christian's personal faith but the faith of the whole Church, which as the believing community has being and continuity in time and space. This believing community is prior to the personal life of the believer, since it already exists when he is born into it by baptism. Infant baptism is prized by Bonhoeffer precisely because it expresses this priority and givenness of the Church.[69]

Bonhoeffer was critical of the early Barth for his congregationalist ecclesiology, stressing act over being. Barth, of course, has since shifted his position considerably, allowing greater room in his theology for the immanence of God in Christ.[70] Barth appears to have accepted, in large measure, Bonhoeffer's Lutheran principle of *finitum capax infiniti* over against the Calvinistic *non capax*, and yet his doctrine of the Church still leaves much to be desired from the standpoint of Bonhoeffer's concern for the unity of act and being. Barth continues to conceive of the Church in wholly actualistic terms, as an event in which two or three are gathered together in the name of Christ.[71] His rejection of infant baptism and his preference for a purely congregational church order are also highly significant.

Bishop Robinson, of course, stands closer to Bonhoeffer than to

[68] Interview, December 29, 1964.

[69] Cf. Bonhoeffer's *Act and Being* (tr. B. Noble), New York: Harper & Brothers, 1962, pp. 111, 121, 128, and 133.

[70] Cf. *The Humanity of God* (tr. J. T. Thomas), Richmond: John Knox Press, 1960, pp. 37–65.

[71] 'The Living Congregation of the Living Lord Jesus Christ', in *Man's Disorder and God's Design*, London: SCM Press, 1948; cited by F. Sherman, 'Act and Being', in *The Place of Bonhoeffer: Problems and Possibilities in his Thought* (ed. M. Marty), London: SCM Press, 1963, p. 106; cf. also *The Humanity of God*, p. 63.

Barth. He would preserve, to use Bonhoeffer's terminology, the actuality and being of the Church, for this secular community (act) is both the Body of Christ and the eschatological community (being). Bonhoeffer, however, never developed a systematic ecclesiology of his own, and it would be totally erroneous to suppose that Robinson simply used and followed him as a pattern and guide. Bonhoeffer's ecclesiology, despite certain variations, was essentially Lutheran; Bishop Robinson's, with similar qualifications, is essentially Anglican. Hence, the two would differ accordingly on such fundamental questions as the Church as the Body of Christ, the relationship of the Church to the preached Word and the act of faith, and especially the ministry of the Church and the episcopacy in particular. Bonhoeffer, in fact, plays no significant role in Robinson's understanding of the Church's nature (in the sense that we have discussed it in the preceding chapters). It is in the post-Cambridge years, as Bishop of Woolwich with definite pastoral responsibilities, that Robinson turns to the martyred Lutheran theologian. And he turns to Bonhoeffer, not to adopt a systematic framework from which to work (for none exists in Bonhoeffer's writings – and least of all in his *Letters and Papers from Prison* which is, for all practical purposes, *the* source for Robinson), but to acquire and implement a spirit. The Church, as Christ, must exist for others. The Church in the world must be the Servant and not the Lord.[72] She must interpret and execute her mission in the light of these principles.

What is to be said of Robinson's use of Bonhoeffer?[73] First of all,

[72] This does not mean, however, that there exists a theological antithesis between the role of the Servant and that of the King. Following Tillich, Robinson agrees that the Church has a royal as well as a priestly and a prophetic office. 'No position can be, or has been, so easily abused. But this does not release the Servant from responsibility.' And then quoting Tillich: 'As the royal function belongs to the Christ Crucified, so the royal function must be exercised by the Church under the Cross, the humble church.' 'It is fully compatible', Bishop Robinson concludes, 'with the proper humiliation of the Church' (*The New Reformation?*, p. 30 and n. 2).

[73] We are limiting our question to the development of the notion of the Servant Church and the Church as secular community. The same question will have to be raised again in the next chapter with reference to the notion of the Church as missionary community and specifically with regard to her mission to preach the gospel to all mankind.

Bonhoeffer's basic insight (as Christ existed as 'the man for others', so, too, must the Church exist to serve humanity) is theologically sound and pastorally important. We shall see further on in this chapter that the notion of the Servant Church is not limited to Protestant theology, but has been adopted and developed, albeit in a limited fashion thus far, by Catholic theologians as well and is, at least implicitly, the prevailing perspective of the *De Ecclesia* constitution of the Second Vatican Council. Secondly, Robinson's use of Bonhoeffer is judicious and moderate. The bishop's distinctive spirit of 'comprehensiveness', so characteristic of Anglicanism, appears to have safeguarded him from any uncritical and uniform acceptance of Bonhoeffer's ecclesiological position. It is a 'comprehensiveness' that allows him to incorporate, even in this one particular area of his doctrine of the Church, such apparently disparate elements as Cullmann, Tillich, and (as we shall see) Congar. Bonhoeffer occupies a central place, but he shares the theological 'spot-light', so to speak, with others of equal or even greater stature.

A fourth major source of Robinson's concept of the Servant Church is corporate rather than individual. It is corporate in the sense that it embraces a number of various sociological, rather than specifically theological, sources. A casual perusal of the footnotes of either *Honest to God* or *The New Reformation?* would clearly disclose his frequent and heavy reliance upon works of a practical and empirical nature as well as those of a more theoretical, yet still sociological, nature. Two of the more prominent religious sociologists whom Robinson has chosen to draw upon in recent years are Gibson Winter[74] and Peter Berger.[75] The latter author is particularly relevant here because he is a theologically alert Lutheran in the Bonhoeffer tradition.

Winter sees the prophetic fellowship (over against the medieval idea of the Church as the cultic organism or the Reformation model of the confessional assembly) as the only relevant form of the Servant Church in a secularized world. The implementation of this

[74] Cf. *The Suburban Captivity of the Churches*, New York: Doubleday, 1961, and *The New Creation as Metropolis*, New York: Macmillan, 1963.

[75] Cf. *The Noise of Solemn Assemblies: Christian Commitment and the Religious Establishment in America*, New York: Doubleday, 1961, and *The Precarious Vision: A Sociologist Looks at Social Fictions and Christian Faith*, New York: Doubleday, 1961.

principle would demand nothing less than an institutional revolution
for the Church. Evangelical centres and academies must replace the
residential churches in the new society. The division between clergy
and laity must be re-evaluated in the light of the fact that the
ministry in the Servant Church is the work of the laity in the world
with auxiliary help from theological specialists. Preaching would no
longer be the preserve of the clergy, but would become the layman's
task within the worldly structures in which he lives and works. So
too must the liturgical life of the Church become integral to the
ministry of the laity and not confined to the 'cultic moment' in the
congregational assembly.[76]

Robinson expresses sympathy for these ideas because they seem to
point in the right direction at least. However, he is careful to formulate
certain reservations with which we can only concur; namely, the
simple identification of the Church with the evangelical centres and
academies cannot be sustained, and, in fact, no real reform can be
expected to take root 'in isolation from the traditional centres of
theological engagement, the councils of the Church, the religious
communities, the universities and the seminaries. For unless it is
planted in these and can draw upon their resources, it will be stunted
for lack of depth of earth.'[77]

The vision and perspective of Peter Berger is captured by the
quotation from the book of Amos which serves to set the tone of his
first monograph, *The Noise of Solemn Assemblies: Christian Commitment
and the Religious Establishment in America*:

> I hate, I despise your feasts, and I take no delight in your solemn
> assemblies.
> Even though you offer me your burnt offerings and cereal offerings,
> I will not accept them, and the peace offerings of your fatted beasts
> I will not look upon.
> Take away from me the noise of your songs: to the melody of your
> harps I will not listen.
> But let justice roll down like waters, and righteousness like an
> ever-flowing stream (5.21–24, RSV).

For Berger the social relevance of the Christian community is not

[76] Cf. Robinson's own summary and analysis, *The New Reformation?*, pp. 64–66.
[77] *Ibid.*, p. 66.

a political imperative but an imperative only of the Christian faith. 'It is the nature of the Christian faith, not the nature of society, which calls for the prophetic mission of the Christian community. Christians are called to be the salt of the earth. If they cease to be that, they risk betraying the very purpose of the Church of Jesus Christ.'[78] He lists four major possibilities of social engagement in the world: (1) Christian diaconate, which is 'the helping outreach of the Christian community to individuals in distress – those suffering from illness, poverty, or other personal difficulties';[79] (2) Christian action, which is 'any attempt not only to deal with individuals but also to try to modify the social structure itself';[80] (3) Christian presence, which may be defined as 'the erection of Christian signs in the world' such as was envisaged by Charles de Foucauld in founding the Little Brothers of Jesus;[81] and (4) Christian dialogue, which is 'the attempt to engage the Christian faith in conversation with the world'.[82] This is the 'academy' approach mentioned above by G. Winter. The Church will be able to engage in these areas of secular mission only to the extent that she can free herself from the bondage of the taken-for-granted religious establishment. Here the distinction between 'religion' and authentic Christian faith as proposed by Bonhoeffer is central to Berger's argument. 'Religion', he contends, 'functions sociologically to represent the integration of the society. Religion may then function psychologically as a "socializing agency", that is, to assist the individual to adjust to this society and to be happy in the process.'[83] Religion, therefore, serves as a major obstacle to authenticity. It prevents the person from seeing himself objectively, apart from the routines of his everyday life. In fact, 'it ratifies the routines, sanctifies the values by which the social roles are rationalized, comforts the individual if personal crises threaten his social adjustment'.[84] Thus, *the social irrelevance of the religious establishment is its functionality*.[85]

The main thrust of Berger's thesis is carried through in his second book, *The Precarious Vision: A Sociologist Looks at Social Fictions and*

---

[78] *The Noise of Solemn Assemblies*, p. 138.
[79] *Ibid.*, p. 140.   [80] *Ibid.*, pp. 144–145.   [81] *Ibid.*, p. 147.
[82] *Ibid.*, p. 149.
[83] *Ibid.*, p. 97.   [84] *Ibid.*, p. 103.   [85] *Idem, loc. cit.*

Christian Faith, wherein he reasserts his conviction 'that the preponderant tendency of religion is to be socially functional rather than disfunctional. That is, religion will tend to provide integrating symbols rather than symbols of revolution. Religion will tend to legitimate power rather than to put it in question. Religion will tend to find rationalizations for social inequalities (both among the beneficiaries and the injured in these arrangements) rather than to seek their removal.'[86] Religion ratifies what he calls the 'okay world', and in doing so religion contributes to bad faith because in reality man does not live in an 'okay world' at all. Accepting Bonhoeffer's anti-religious critique and his analysis of the 'world come of age', Berger synthesizes his own position in this way:

> The natural inclinations of man lead him to take society for granted, to identify himself fully with the social roles assigned to him, and to develop ideologies which will organize and dispose of any doubts that might possibly arise. There is an instructive affinity between Christian faith and the analytical enterprise of the social sciences in that both serve to disturb this happy state of affairs. The Christian faith, in its prophetic mission, confronts man with a truth of such force that the precarious pretensions of his social existence disintegrate before it. The debunking effect of social-scientific analysis is far from contradictory to this prophetic mission. Indeed, it might be called its profane auxiliary. The smashing of idols, with whatever hammers, is the underside of prophecy.[87]

The above summary serves also as an adequate explanation of Robinson's frequent use of sociological as well as theological sources. The bishop is engaged in a kind of prophetic enterprise and, as Berger clearly indicates, social-scientific analysis is its 'underside'. While it is important, and indeed essential, to take into account the various sociological and other non-theological sources of Robinson's view of the Church's mission, one must be careful to avoid a twofold temptation: (1) to assume that much of Bishop Robinson's ecclesiology is simply empirical in nature, and without serious theological substance; and (2) to overlook the fundamentally critical and judicious use which Robinson makes of these same sources. The material which we examined in the second, third and fourth chapters alone should be sufficient to mitigate the force of the first assumption,

[86] *The Precarious Vision*, p. 111.   [87] *Ibid.*, p. 204.

and his careful handling of both Bonhoeffer and Winter, to cite but two examples, should exclude the second. Robinson's assessment of Berger is completely favourable – to the extent that he makes use of him. But what has been said already of his use of Bonhoeffer would apply equally well to his use of Berger. There is no question, in other words, of a theological *rapprochement* on such fundamental issues as church order, the relationship between the Church and the Word, and so forth. Once again the spirit of 'comprehensiveness' is at work.

A fifth and final source for Robinson's understanding of the Church as a secular community, i.e. *in* this *age* and *for* the world, is Yves M.-J. Congar. It would be more accurate, perhaps, to describe Congar's role as confirmatory rather than derivative. For Bishop Robinson, Congar offers independent support from the Catholic side to Bonhoeffer's concept of authentic Christian worldliness. The Church must become genuinely and increasingly *lay*, Robinson has argued in his most recent books, but not in the sense of abolishing its sacramental ministers or of making the Church a lay movement. Rather it is a question of perspective, of seeing the laity for what they really are; namely, the *laos* or people of God *in the world*.[88] Robinson's assessment – and use – of Congar is most evident in his essay, 'The Ministry and the Laity', where he writes:

> The designation that for me goes nearer to the heart of the matter than any other is that given in pages 17–22 of Father Yves Congar's great book, *Lay People in the Church*. The layman, he says, is one for whom the things of this world really exist for their own sake; their truth is not, as it were, swallowed up and destroyed by a higher reference, so that everything has first to become religious in order to be interesting, and the secular is important and relevant only if it can somehow be turned to the service of the Church or violently baptized into Christ. And this temper of mind, what Congar calls 'a genuine laicity', need not, and must not, be confined to those not ordained. It is a temper which should characterize the entire Church. It is what Dietrich Bonhoeffer was pleading for in his call for an authentic Christian worldliness.[89]

[88] Cf. *The New Reformation?*, chapter 3: 'Towards a Genuinely Lay Theology', wherein the bishop makes use of other Catholic sources, such as Charles Davis.
[89] 'The Ministry and the Laity', p. 18, cf. also *Honest to God*, p. 137; *The World that God Loves*, p. 6.

For the moment it is enough to say that Robinson is faithful to Congar's thought. However, in the third and final section of this chapter we shall consider certain other writings of the French Dominican which did not come to the bishop's attention. The re-examination of the Church-and-world relationship has not at all been confined to Bonhoeffer and his 'school', but rather has been a source of serious concern for theologians of the Catholic tradition, including K. Rahner and E. Schillebeeckx. In addition to these theologians, the service orientation of the Christian ministry is clearly indicated in the *De Ecclesia* constitution of the Second Vatican Council, and a more detailed elaboration of this Church-and-world relationship is found in the Council's *Pastoral Constitution on the Church in the Modern World* (fourth session).

THE SERVANT CHURCH IN CONTEMPORARY CATHOLIC THEOLOGY

Yves Congar is the Catholic ecclesiologist who, among all contemporary Catholic theologians, has written most extensively – and most perceptively – on the place and mission of the Church in the modern world. An examination, however brief, of Congar's theological position will serve to set in relief what deficiencies exist in Bishop Robinson's conception of the Church's mission in the world. And if there is any one particular failing in Robinson's construction, it is the certain measure of superficiality that pervades his writings in this area of his theology of the Church. For Congar, unlike Robinson, explores the ultimate theological foundation of the Church's mission in explicit terms. Whereas the bishop is apparently content to state that the Church's mission is to be the Son of Man on earth rather than examine in some detail the essential connection between the mission of Christ and the mission of the Church (and, more specifically even, the mission of the Apostles), Congar insists first of all upon this fundamental relationship (cf. John 20.21; 17.18) and indicates that both together constitute a mission of love (cf. John 3.16; I John 4.9). The agents of this mission are the Holy Spirit and the apostolic ministry (cf. John 14; 16; 17), for the Spirit is sent to actualize inwardly what the Lord had instituted outwardly

(Acts 1.1–2; 20.28). The mission of the Twelve has priority, but the Spirit was both promised and sent to all the faithful (Mark 13.11, etc.). The faithful are the living stones and part of the Temple (I Cor. 3.16–17; Eph. 2.21–22; I Peter 2.5, etc.), but, unlike the Apostles, they are neither the master-builders (I Cor. 3.9–17) nor the foundation (Eph. 2.20). Apostolicity, on the other hand, is an organic function, a service, a ministry existing for the Body, for a house is not a house without a superstructure.[90]

But the Church's mission is not simply inner-directed and Church-centred. 'Pentecost', Congar suggests, 'was, precisely, the placing of the Church in the world.'[91] It represents the bursting asunder of Jerusalem and the inauguration of the mission of universalism. But, again, the mission is not general or vague; it is a mission of the Spirit (John 14.16, 26; 15.16) and of the Apostles (John 13.16, 20; 17.18). The Apostles are called separately and then collectively designated as such, and then Peter is set apart (Matt. 16.17–19). They are given special instructions and special powers (Luke 9.1 ff.; Matt. 16.19–20; 18.18, etc.). They are actually sent (John 17.16–18; 13.20; 15.18–21, 23; 16.2–3; 17.19, etc.). For as the Father has sent the Son, so has the Son sent the Apostles (John 17.18, 22–23; 20.21). 'The persistence of the mission,' Congar writes, 'which assures the movement of *agape* on the part of God towards men is shown by the fact that the one sent and the person sending are equal in dignity, which is expressed in the Aramaic word for sent, *Saliah*. The one sent represents the person of his master and has the same authority; he is to be received in the same way as the master himself, from whom he has a power of attorney and whose functions he exercises in his absence. This is, undoubtedly, the whole idea of the apostolate instituted by Christ (cf. John 13.16, 20; 15.20; 17.9 ff., esp. 18; also Luke 10.16; Matt. 10.40).'[92]

The sending of the Spirit, on the other hand, follows the exaltation of Jesus as Lord. The Spirit's is a mission distinct from Christ's, whereas that of the Apostles is but the continuation of Christ's. The

[90] Cf. *Lay People in the Church*, chapter 5, pp. 333–378; cf. also pp. 429–436.
[91] *The Mystery of the Church* (tr. A. V. Littledale), Baltimore: Helicon, 1960, p. 42.
[92] *Ibid.*, p. 149.

Spirit works to apply what Christ has accomplished and established and to bring it to its ultimate completion. To fulfil this function the Spirit is sent by the Father at the request and in the name of the Son (John 14; 16.26) and is sometimes sent by Christ himself (John 15.26; 16.7; Luke 24.49; Acts 2.33). This dependence in the sphere of the temporal economy supposes a dependence in the mystery of the Trinity itself. 'It has often been observed', Congar notes, 'that a theology which denies the eternal procession of the Holy Spirit from the Word tends to minimize the part played by definite forms of authority in actual life, and leaves the way more open to a kind of independent inspiration.'[93]

Congar summarizes his discussion in this way:

> There is a duality of agents (or of missions) that realize the work of Christ, the Spirit working internally, with a divine efficaciousness, what the apostolic ministry effects externally; he himself, to that end, being bound by a bond of alliance, in virtue of God's fidelity to his promises.
>
> The Church owes its structures to the institution of the means of grace, deriving from the *acta Christi in carne*. It is fundamentally Christological.
>
> But it lives, under the government of the glorified Christ, by the action of the Holy Spirit. Its life is thus a sphere in which the transcendence of its Head and the personality, equally transcendent, of the Spirit, are manifested in the sovereign liberty of their gifts and interventions.[94]

The Church, although she has existence in herself, does not exist for herself. She is essentially missionary, and her mission is hierarchically structured in the Spirit. Not only must she preach the

---

[93] *The Mystery of the Church*, p. 153.

[94] *Ibid.*, p. 116; cf. also *The Mystery of the Temple: The Manner of God's Presence to His Creatures from Genesis to the Apocalypse* (tr. R. Trevett), London: Burns & Oates, 1962, pp. 154 ff., and 284 ff., and *Les voies du Dieu vivant: Théologie et vie spirituelle*, Paris: Cerf, 1962, pp. 165–184 ('L'Esprit-Saint dans l'Eglise'). Cf. also R. Schnackenburg, *Die Kirche im Neuen Testament*, pp. 15–17, 53–58, 140–146; cf. also pp. 46–51, 122–126, and 156–165; and C. Journet, *L'Eglise du Verbe Incarné*, vol. II, pp. 1224–1225. The role of the Spirit in the mission of the Church is also discussed from a different point of view by H. Conzelmann, *The Theology of St Luke* (tr. G. Buswell), London: Faber & Faber, 1961, pp. 123–136; and E. Schweizer, *Spirit of God* (tr. A. E. Harvey) in *Bible Key Words* (*ThWNT*), London: A. & C. Black, 1960; cf. also his *Church Order in the New Testament*, p. 95.

Gospel to make disciples of all nations, but she must also tend to 'the preambles to apostleship', for before one can be a Christian and acknowledge the Lordship of Christ, one must first be a man. The Church, therefore, cannot neglect her mission 'to form man in his fullness and so ceaselessly to collaborate in building the solid basis of society. This mission is of her essence.'[95] For according to the Gospel discipleship necessarily involves a spirit and works of service to others. To be a disciple and to be a servant, *mathetes* and *diakonos*, are bound up together, and they diminish or increase together (cf. I Cor. 9.19–22; II Cor. 4.5; Gal. 5.13).[96]

It follows, then, that the hierarchical ministry is to be viewed and exercised in the context of service, and this is a theme that runs throughout Christian tradition. The New Testament witness is clear. The 'greatest in the Kingdom of Heaven' is the one who humbles himself like a child (Matt. 18.4). When dealing with the question of precedence in the Kingdom as raised by the mother of Jesus and John, Jesus taught that one who wishes to be great must be the servant, 'and whoever wants to be first must be the willing slave of all. For even the Son of Man did not come to be served but to serve, and to surrender his life as a ransom for many' (Mark 10.43–45; cf. Matt. 20.25–28). Indeed, *diakonia* is practically co-extensive and identical with the character of the disciple throughout the New Testament (cf. Phil. 2.6–11; John 13.12–13; II Cor. 4.5; 1.24; I Peter 5.3; John 10.10 f.). But, according to Congar, we are still a long way from the goal of de-clericalizing our conception of the Church (without, of course, jeopardizing her hierarchical structure) and placing the clergy in proper perspective, that is to say, as member-servants.[97]

The Church is the community of those who acknowledge the Lordship of Christ, a community-in-the-Spirit and hierarchically structured, which has a mission to the world, a mission to preach the gospel and also to build up the community of mankind. The Church, therefore, does not exist for herself alone, but for the Kingdom and for the world. Thus, her entire ministry is to be seen as a ministry of

---

[95] *Laity, Church and World* (tr. D. Attwater), Baltimore: Helicon, 1960, p. 49.

[96] *Ibid.*, cf. p. 63; cf. also *Lay People in the Church*, pp. 366–367.

[97] Cf. *Power and Poverty in the Church*, pp. 17 ff., and 139.

service, of *diakonia*, as well as of witnessing, of *marturia*. Yet how are
we to evaluate the success of the Church's mission? Must not the
Church build up her own structures and enlarge her own membership even as she is exercising her ministry of witness and service?
What is to be said, in other words, of the minority status of the
Church in the world? Congar treats this problem in the light of the
Bible, and his judgement, in brief, is that the category of quantity is
unimportant to the Bible, that the Church is a minority in the service
of the majority. The Bible is not concerned with numbers as such.
Its thought is 'all-embracing', that is to say, 'it includes the particular
in the whole, whether as seed, root or fruit of a tree'.[98] Thus, mankind
is chosen to represent the world in giving God the praise of all
creation; Israel is chosen for mankind, to be God's witness and priest
among men; and as for Israel, so for the Church. 'It is to Christians
that we have to apply the idea of being the dynamic representative
minority that is spiritually responsible for the final destiny of all.'[99]
Indeed, the Christian doctrine of Redemption cannot be understood
apart from this biblical idea of 'representative inclusion'. Furthermore, these ideas of totality and representative value are joined
together in the typically biblical notion of first-fruits. The Christians
are the first-fruits of all creation (James 1.18); Christ is the first-
fruits of the Resurrection (I Cor. 15.20, 23). The Church is truly 'a
small Church in a large world', but whose minority status is not a
scandal.[100]

Karl Rahner discusses the very same question in his suggestive
essay, 'A Theological Interpretation of the Position of Christians in
the Modern World'.[101] It would be appropriate to note here, at the

---

[98] *The Wide World My Parish*, p. 11.   [99] *Ibid.*, p. 12.

[100] Cf. Congar's comparison of the Church's activity to that of the French
underground during the Second World War: *ibid.*, pp. 25–26. I have developed
this same theme elsewhere: *Clergy Review*, *art. cit.* I am not aware of any other
Catholic attempt to develop in such a specific manner the theological notion
of the Church as Servant of God in the world. The argument was taken up most
notably at the Second Vatican Council by Cardinal Valerian Gracias, Archbishop of Bombay: 'Not Domination but Service', in *Council Speeches of Vatican II*
(ed. H. Kung, Y. Congar, D. O'Hanlon), pp. 284–288. Bishop Robinson accepts
and employs my view in *The New Reformation?*, p. 49.

[101] *Mission and Grace* (tr. C. Hastings), vol. I, London: Sheed & Ward, 1963,
pp. 3–55.

outset, that this particular contribution of Rahner's did not come to Bishop Robinson's attention. While the conclusions of the two authors are in basic agreement, Robinson reaches his without the benefit of Rahner's theological groundwork, and to that extent suffers from a certain measure of superficiality.

The Church, Rahner argues, finds itself in a *diaspora* situation today, and this is a condition to which she must simply adjust; for in terms of the history of salvation this situation signifies a 'must' from which we may and must draw conclusions about our behaviour as Christians. There are some things that 'ought' to be, and others that 'simply are'. At first glance, it would seem that the Church 'ought' to be in a position of supreme social and cultural influence in the world, that she 'simply is not' but must strive to be so. Yet, for Rahner, there is a third possibility; namely, things that 'ought not to be' yet 'must' be so. Thus, they are not simply to be endured or protested against, but are to be given their due. These things, precisely as existing (and not simply as something to be grimly endured or fought against), have a significance for salvation. This is certainly the witness of Scripture: 'the poor you will always have with you' (Matt. 26.11); the inevitability of scandals and schisms (cf. John 16.1–5); and the supreme instance, the Cross itself. 'Hence,' Rahner concludes, 'it is possible and permissible for a Christian to affirm a "must" of this sort within the history of salvation, to reckon with it as such, and to draw from it conclusions involving an "ought" for his own conduct, even though it does not itself arise from any *a priori* "ought", but from historical causes and even from human guilt and failure. . . . [Therefore] we have not only to acknowledge this *diaspora* situation as unfortunately permitted by God, but can recognize it as willed by God as a "must" (not as an "ought") and go freely on to draw our conclusions from it.'[102]

With the possible exception of Spain and Portugal, there are no more Christian countries. Christians exist everywhere in *diaspora* and as a minority. The situation is not getting better; it is getting worse. It 'ought not to be', that is to say, all men should have accepted Christ once he has been preached to them, but it 'must' be so. Christ promised to be with his Church always, and yet he also warned

[102] *Mission and Grace*, pp. 21–23.

that his work would always be a sign of contradiction and persecution, of dire and desperate combat; that the love of Christians would
grow cold; and that only a progressive leavening process would lead
up to the act of God coming in judgement to gather up world history
and its wholly unpredictable and unexpected end. During the
medieval period the Church was a community gathered against the
outside world. The enemy was always outside its ranks. But the old
world order disintegrated in the face of the Reformation, the
Renaissance, the Enlightenment, the French Revolution. The Church
was no longer the Church of a closed culture. When medieval culture
became the vehicle for world-wide expansion, the Church moved
with it into the world at large. 'In the moment when she begins to be
a Church of *all* the heathen, she also begins, everywhere, to be a
Church *among the heathen*.'[103] The Church is in a *diaspora* situation,
and this is a 'must' in the history of salvation.

What are the elements of this *diaspora* situation? (1) The faith of
the Christian is under constant threat, for there is little or no
institutional support. It is a matter now of personal choice and
decision rather than natural sociological growth. (2) A considerable
part of the cultural milieu (literary, artistic, and scientific) will not
be specifically Christian or bear the stamp of the Christian gospel.
(3) The Church is a community of active members, and not simply
a clerical enterprise. The Church will gradually acquire a certain
sectarian character (sociologically) and will no longer be able to
exercise all the functions which it once did. The Church of the
diaspora will be more immediately religious. (4) The clergy will no
longer be automatically in a privileged position in society (again, in
terms of social status). (5) There will be fewer confrontations
between Church and State. In the past all were members of both.
In the future this will not be so.[104]

What are the consequences of this new situation? 'Though we
must keep our missionary fervour, there is nevertheless a right sense
in which we must adjust ourselves to the *diaspora* situation and come
to terms with it. . . . [This principle] makes us realize that there
can be points over which we do *not* need to take the offensive, where
we can let things take their course and come to terms with them,

[103] *Mission and Grace*, pp. 29–30.   [104] *Ibid.*, cf. pp. 33–39.

precisely so as to work away with all our available and limited resources, interior and exterior, at other points where it makes sense to do so, and thus not waste our energies in the wrong place.'[105]

Thus, he argues against such goals as Catholic universities and government legislation on morality. The Christian must be more tolerant of environmental influences in shaping the moral attitudes of the non-Christian. Pastors must be conscious of serving people and not an impersonal institution. In everything we say or write we must always be aware of the non-Christian. Is this simply a question of resignation and defeat? Not at all! 'Just where is it written that *we* must have the whole 100%? God must have all, we hope that he takes pity on all and will have all indeed. But we cannot say that he is doing so only if we, meaning the Church, have everybody. . . . In short, if we demanded less of ourselves, but that less the right thing, i.e. not universal Christianity, when the *diaspora* is an inescapable "must", but a battle for new individuals, then, though immediate statistics would not look any better, the real state of our mission, in respect of its chance for the future, would surely be improved. Then we should realize in practice, not only in theory, that even in the *diaspora* the initiative can really be ours.'[106]

The concept of the Church as secular community is also endorsed by E. Schillebeeckx. The Church is a communion in grace and a visible sign, or sacrament, of the grace of Christ. As such this community has been commissioned by Christ to open the world 'to receive the Good Tidings, and, by speaking this Word, incarnating it in the world as a foretaste of the eschatological glorification of the body and of the "new heaven and earth".'[107] This mission is given to a community which is intimately involved in this world, which means that 'the *typical* mark of the Christian lay status will be an apostolate carried on in and through direct concern with secular affairs'.[108] 'It is precisely because the layman *personally shares*, through grace, in God's own creative love for the world, that he

---

[105] *Mission and Grace*, pp. 40–41.

[106] *Ibid.*, pp. 51–52. For a strongly divergent view, cf. J. Daniélou, 'Little Flock or Great People?', *Furrow* 15 (1964) 757–761.

[107] 'The Layman in the Church', in *Vatican II: The Struggle of Minds and other essays*, Dublin: M. H. Gill, 1963, p. 47.

[108] *Ibid.*, p. 41.

becomes conscious . . . that his secular occupation has a positive, divine, redemptive sense, a significance in the economy of salvation.'[109] The institutional Church, therefore, must not consider itself as an end, but 'an instrument in the hands of Christ, at the service of all mankind, in and through her real and realistic faith in the coming of the Kingdom of God'.[110]

Finally, the general lines of thought traced throughout this present chapter are corroborated, at least implicitly, by the teaching of the Second Vatican Council, although the major portion of its task remains unfinished business. First of all, the Council declares that the Spirit is the source of the Church's mission in the world[111] and that this mission-in-the-Spirit is conferred by Christ upon his Apostles.[112] The Spirit and the hierarchical structure are the two essential elements. Secondly, the Council lays continual stress, in its treatment of the various levels of ministry within the Church, on the service-orientation that each must have: the episcopacy,[113] the priesthood,[114] and the diaconate.[115] And, thirdly, the Council notes that the laity is specifically characterized by a secular calling, [116] that as members of the messianic People of God they are sent forth into the whole world as the light of the world and the salt of the earth. Although this community does not actually include all men, and at times may look like a small flock, it is none the less a lasting and sure seed of unity, hope and salvation for the whole human race.[117]

Our consideration of the current situation in Catholic theology, from Congar to the Second Vatican Council has been designed to serve a twofold purpose. First, this comparative study illuminates certain weaknesses – or, perhaps better, certain *underdeveloped* areas – in the argumentation of Bishop Robinson; namely, his failure to explore in sufficient depth the relationship of the Holy Spirit and the apostolic college to the mission of the Church. Secondly, an examination of these writings, and especially those of Congar and Rahner, clearly indicates that this kind of theological speculation

[109] 'The Layman in the Church', p. 50.
[110] *The National Catholic Reporter*, vol. 1, no. 4, November 18, 1964, p. 2: cf. also his 'The Church and Mankind', *Concilium* 1 (1965) 34–50.
[111] *De Ecclesia*, I, 4.
[112] *Ibid.*, III, *passim.*   [113] *Ibid.*, III, 20.   [114] *Ibid.*, III, 28.
[115] *Ibid.*, III, 29.   [116] *Ibid.*, IV, 31.   [117] *Ibid.*, II, 9.

knows no Reformation barriers. The concerns are identical and, in most of the cases analysed, so, too, are the conclusions. How is the Church to fulfil her mission in the modern world, a world industrialized, urbanized and – most importantly – secularized? Indeed, what is the mission of the Church? Is it simply to preach the Gospel, without particular concern for the mode of expression or the actual effects (as Barth and, to an extent, Cullmann have suggested)? Does her mission merely consist in outward expansion so as to grow and increase numerically in time and in space (as, perhaps, many Christians on both sides of the Reformation-divide believe)? Or does the Church exist as Servant of God and Son of Man on earth, as a Church in *diaspora*, as the *secular community?* John A. T. Robinson, under the impact of pastoral responsibility and especially since his consecration in 1959, has clearly aligned himself with those who propose the last thesis. In so doing he has placed himself in an ever-widening stream of Protestant theological thought which claims Dietrich Bonhoeffer as its source.[118] In recent years there has been a convergence of this stream with another of a Catholic nature, that of Congar and Rahner in particular. For reasons outlined in this chapter, and elsewhere,[119] these currents – in our judgement – are flowing in the right direction.

[118] For an accurate indication of the new thinking at the World Council of Churches with regard to this central question of the Church's mission in the world, cf. Colin W. Williams, *Where in the World?: Changing Forms of the Church's Witness*, New York: The National Council of the Churches of Christ, 1963, and *What in the World?* published in 1964 by the same organization (both books also published by Epworth Press, London, 1965). Bishop Robinson refers to Williams' works as a 'brilliant' summary in popular form of the pertinent issues involved. Cf. *The New Reformation?*, p. 88. And in a letter to me (June 15, 1965) the bishop wrote: 'I regard the new thinking that is being fed in from this source as every bit as important as what is coming from the Vatican Council – and, if I may say so, it is a good deal more radical!'

[119] *Clergy Review, art. cit.*

6

THE CHURCH:
THE MISSIONARY COMMUNITY

STATE OF THE QUESTION

WHILE there may exist differences of views on the notion of the Servant Church, or the Church as the secular community, it seems to be an incontrovertible theological fact that the Church is, in one way or another, a *missionary* community, i.e. a community with a mandate to preach the gospel to all mankind. 'Go forth therefore and make all nations my disciples,' the classical text reads; 'baptize men everywhere in the name of the Father and the Son and the Holy Spirit, and teach them to observe all that I have commanded you' (Matt. 28.19–20).

Oscar Cullmann voices the consensus on this point when he writes:

It is the action of the Holy Spirit which makes the action of the Church, as such, eschatological. The Church itself is an eschatological phenomenon. It is the centre of the present lordship of Christ. It was constituted by the Holy Spirit at Pentecost. That is why the task of the Church consists in the proclamation of the Gospel to the whole world. This is the very essence of the Holy Spirit's work, and the meaning of the miracle at Pentecost, when, quite suddenly, all present understood each other. Precisely in the period to which we belong – between the resurrection and the return of Christ – it is the duty of the Church to go out 'into all the world and preach the Gospel to every creature', looking towards the end.[1]

[1] 'Eschatology and Missions in the New Testament', in the Dodd *Festschrift*, pp. 412–413. Cf. also his 'Kingship of Christ and the Church in the New Testament', pp. 133 ff., and *Christ and Time* (1956), pp. 157 ff. Cf. also E. Schweizer, *Spirit of God*, pp. 42–43.

This has always been the position of Catholic theology and doctrine. The *De Ecclesia* constitution of the Second Vatican Council represents its most recent formulation. Commenting upon the classical text quoted above, the Council declared:

> The Church has received from the Apostles this solemn mandate of Christ to proclaim the saving truth and must carry it out to the very ends of the earth (cf. Acts 1.8), wherefore she makes the words of the Apostle her own: 'Woe to me, if I do not preach the gospel' (I Cor. 9.16), and continues unceasingly to send heralds of the gospel until such time as the infant churches are fully established and can themselves continue the work of evangelizing. . . . By the proclamation of the gospel she prepares her hearers to receive and profess the faith. She gives them the dispositions necessary for baptism, snatches them from the slavery of error and of idols, and incorporates them in Christ so that through charity they may grow up into full maturity in Christ.[2]

The Catholic Church has always regarded this mission as an essential function and has, in every period of her history, sent missionaries into non-Christian lands to make the message of Christ available to all. It is only in recent decades, under the impact of secularization, that the Church has conceived her mission not only in terms of preaching the gospel to the pagans in distant lands, but more especially in terms of preaching the gospel to the dechristianized, to those who have had the gospel preached to them but who no longer listen to it.

The notion of the Church's mission has undergone a similar, although by no means identical, development among the Protestants. The fundamental opposition of both Luther and Calvin to the missionary work of the Church is well known. Until the second half of the nineteenth century both Lutheranism and Calvinism adhered firmly to the theological views of their respective founders. Since then there has been a re-awakening of missionary consciousness among the various Protestant communities. In 1961 at New Delhi

[2] II, 17; cf. also II, 13; III, 19-20; *De Sacra Liturgia*, I, 6; and *De Activitate Missionili Ecclesiae* (Decree on the Mission Activity of the Church—fourth session). It should be noted, of course, that the conception of the Second Vatican Council and that of Cullmann differ essentially from that of Protestants in general; namely, that the Church's mission rests not only upon the Word but also upon the Sacraments (the Eucharist, in particular) and therefore upon the apostolic college as an essential foundation.

the International Missionary Council, which had been established in 1921 and had been convened periodically since then, merged completely with the World Council of Churches.

The stimulus for these new missionary efforts had come from the challenge of secularization, a social phenomenon that had developed from the Renaissance of the fifteenth century, through the period of the Reformation, the Enlightenment, and finally the period of vast economic and cultural change in the late nineteenth and early twentieth centuries. The secular world gradually asserted its autonomy *vis-à-vis* religion in general and the Church in particular. The initial reaction of the Church was defensive and hostile, but in the pontificate of Leo XIII an attempt was made to come to grips with the social upheaval and the new secular spirit. The response offered at the level of social reform proved more imaginative than that proposed in the theological sphere, for this was also the period of the Modernist crisis. It is only in the most recent years, and especially since the Second World War, that the problem of secularization has been confronted openly and with some imagination: 'How are we to preach the gospel to the modern world?' 'How is Christ to be Lord of a world that has come of age?'

'The great problem of the Church (and therefore of its theologians)', H. E. Root has observed, 'is to establish or re-establish some kind of vital contact with that enormous majority of human beings for whom Christian faith is not so much unlikely as irrelevant and uninteresting.'[3]

Those Protestant theologians who have addressed themselves to this problem are an impressive array indeed: Barth, Bultmann, Tillich and Bonhoeffer. It was Karl Barth in his *Commentary on the Epistle of the Romans* who first called into question the assumptions of the liberal theology of the nineteenth and early twentieth centuries. It was Barth, as Bonhoeffer himself admitted,[4] who was the

[3] 'Beginning All Over Again,' in *Soundings*, p. 6; cf. also C. Davis, 'Theology and its Present Task,' in *Theology and the University: an ecumenical investigation* (ed. J. Coulson), London: Darton, Longman & Todd, 1964, pp. 107–132; 'The Danger of Irrelevance,' in *Theology for Today*, New York: Sheed & Ward, 1962, pp. 12–24; and 'Theology in Seminary Confinement,' in *The Downside Review* 81 (1963) 307–316.

[4] *Letters and Papers from Prison*, cf. pp. 91–92, 95, 109–110.

first to formulate a critique of 'religion', calling the God of Jesus Christ into the lists against it, i.e. '*pneuma* against *sarx*'. But about the time of the publication of his book on Anselm in 1930,[5] Barth entered his post-existentialist stage in which he reacts against the intrusion of philosophy into theology and develops, or retreats into (depending upon one's ultimate judgement of his methodology), a positivism of revelation. 'The question of *language*,' he writes in his pivotal essay, *The Humanity of God*, 'about which one must speak in reference to the so-called "outsiders", is not so burning today as is asserted in various quarters. This is true in the first place because, again thinking in terms of the humanity of God, we cannot at all reckon in a serious way with *real* "outsiders", with a "world come of age", but only with a world which *regards* itself as of age (and proves daily that it is precisely not that). . . . So there must be then no particular language for insiders and outsiders. Both are contemporary men-of-the-world – all of us are.'[6]

Bultmann's programme has been markedly different from Barth's. In an essay appearing in 1941,[7] Bultmann argued that the message of the New Testament must be demythologized and reinterpreted in terms of the existentialist philosophy of Martin Heidegger. Bultmann is concerned about the incomprehensibility to contemporary man of the mythological form in which the kerygma, the apostolic proclamation, is expressed. '*The kerygma is incredible to modern man*,' he wrote, '*for he is convinced that the mythical view of the world is obsolete.* . . . Can Christian preaching expect modern man *to accept the mythical view of the world as true?* To do so would be both senseless and impossible.'[8] He goes on to press for a full-scale revision of the entire theological framework: the Creeds, eschatology, the Spirit, the sacraments, original sin, the atonement, and the resurrec-

[5] *Anselm: Fides Quaerens Intellectum* (tr. I. W. Robertson), London: SCM Press, 1960, and New York: World (Meridian), 1962.

[6] Pp. 58–59; cf. also his *Evangelical Theology: An Introduction* (tr. G. Foley), New York: Doubleday, 1964, especially pp. 11, 44, 80 and 89.

[7] 'New Testament and Mythology,' in *Kerygma and Myth* (ed. H. W. Bartsch; tr. H. W. Bartsch and R. H. Fuller), New York: Harper & Row, 1961, pp. 1–44; cf. also his *Jesus Christ and Mythology*, London: SCM Press, 1960, where his original proposal appears in a more popular form.

[8] 'New Testament and Mythology,' p. 3.

tion.[9] An existentialist interpretation of New Testament mythology remains as the only possible solution.[10]

Also engaged in the work of transforming traditional religious symbolism has been Paul Tillich. His theology, of course, has many similarities to that of Bultmann, particularly in their use of philosophies of an existentialistic strain. Tillich is concerned lest God become but a concept among concepts, an object among objects.[11] On the contrary, God is the 'infinite and inexhaustible depth and ground of all being' and our 'ultimate concern'.[12] Tillich, like Barth, offers his own critique of 'religion', calling it 'the great attempt of man to overcome his anxiety and restlessness and despair, to close the gap within himself, and to reach immortality, spirituality, and perfection'.[13] God is God for us only in so far as we do not possess him. 'When we possess God, we reduce Him to that small thing we knew and grasped of Him; and we make it an idol. Only in idol worship can one believe in the possession of God. There is much of this idolatry among Christians.'[14]

Dietrich Bonhoeffer, who addressed himself to the same problem of understanding the gospel in secular terms, was critical of all three theologians. Barth replaced 'religion' with a 'positivism of revelation', which says, in effect, 'Take it or leave it!' 'Barth and the Confessing Church', Bonhoeffer stated in the outline for the book he never lived to write, 'have encouraged us to entrench ourselves behind the "faith of the Church", and evade the honest question, what is our real and personal belief?'[15] Bultmann, on the other hand, did not go far enough in his programme of demythologization. He should have gone beyond miracles, the ascension, and the like, and demytholo-

[9] 'New Testament and Mythology', cf. pp. 4–8.
[10] *Ibid.*, cf. pp. 15–16; cf. also the excellent critique by L. Malevez, *The Christian Message and Myth: The Theology of Rudolf Bultmann* (tr. O. Wyon), London: SCM Press, 1958, cf. chapter 5, pp. 118–163, and especially pp. 155–156.
[11] Cf. *The Shaking of the Foundations*, London: Pelican, 1962, pp. 52–53.
[12] *Ibid.*, pp. 63–64.
[13] *Ibid.*, p. 102. Of course, Tillich does not accept the theological positivism of Karl Barth. Tillich, in contrast to Barth, sees his whole theology as an 'answering theology' and his 'method of correlation' determines the approach of his whole *Systematic Theology*. Cf. vol. 1, pp. 3–76.
[14] *The Shaking of the Foundations*, p. 153.
[15] *Letters and Papers*, p. 165; cf. also pp. 91–92, 95, 109–110.

gized the 'religious' conceptions themselves. 'You cannot, as Bultmann imagines, separate God and miracles, but you do have to be able to interpret and proclaim *both* of them in a "non-religious" sense.'[16] Ultimately, Bultmann's approach is the liberal one, i.e. 'abridging the Gospel',[17] and it suffers to the extent that he goes off into 'the typical liberal reduction process (the "mythological" elements of Christianity are dropped, and Christianity is reduced to its "essence"). . . . The New Testament is not a mythological garbing of the universal truth; this mythology (resurrection and so on) is the thing itself – but the concepts must be interpreted in such a way as not to make religion a precondition of faith (cf. circumcision in St Paul). Not until that is achieved will, in my opinion, liberal theology be overcome. . . .'[18] Finally, Bonhoeffer criticized Tillich, despite his courageous attempt 'to interpret the evolution of the world itself – against its will – in a religious sense, to give it its whole shape through religion'. But his attempt ran aground when 'the world unseated him and went on by itself: he too sought to understand the world better than it understood itself, but it felt entirely *mis*understood, and rejected the imputation'.[19]

But while Barth, Bultmann, and Tillich all recognized the need for a radical approach, it was Bonhoeffer's *Letters and Papers from Prison* that provided its most powerful expression. The overriding question for Bonhoeffer was, 'What *is* Christianity, and indeed what *is* Christ for us today?'[20] In his view the world is proceeding towards a time of no religion at all, and yet, in his judgement, 'our whole nineteen-hundred-year-old Christian preaching and theology rests upon the "religious premise" of man'.[21] Christ must become the Lord even of those who have no religion, and this is possible because 'religion' as such is only the garb of Christianity.

In the past the Church attempted to convince men of their need for religion as an answer to insecurity, fear, and despair. God had become a 'working hypothesis', a *Deus ex machina*, to explain the inexplicable. Even after the social, economic, cultural, and political revolutions, the Church through her apologetics continued in her

[16] *Letters and Papers*, p. 94.
[17] *Idem, loc. cit.*
[18] *Ibid.*, p. 110.
[19] *Ibid.*, pp. 108–109.
[20] *Ibid.*, p. 91.
[21] *Idem, loc. cit.*

attempt to prove to the world thus come of age that it cannot live without the tutelage of God. For Bonhoeffer, Christian apologetics became an 'attack . . . upon the adulthood of the world',[22] and in a pointless, ignoble, and un-Christian manner.

> Pointless, because it looks to me like an attempt to put a grown-up man back into adolescence, i.e. to make him dependent on things on which he is not in fact dependent any more, thrusting him back into the midst of problems which are in fact not problems for him any more. Ignoble, because this amounts to an effort to exploit the weakness of man for purposes alien to him and not freely subscribed to by him. Un-Christian, because for Christ himself is being substituted one particular stage in the religiousness of man, i.e. a human law.[23]

The 'world's coming of age,' then, is no longer to be an occasion for polemics and apologetics. Salvation is no longer to be interpreted as salvation from cares and need, from fears and longing, from sin and death into a better world beyond the grave. On the contrary, 'the difference between the Christian hope of resurrection and a mythological hope is that the Christian hope sends a man back to his life on earth in a wholly new way which is even more sharply defined than it is in the Old Testament'.[24] The Christian does not seek a refuge from earthly tasks and difficulties but is taken hold of by Christ at the very centre of his life. No longer is God to be considered as a *Deus ex machina*, for the only way to be honest in this entirely new situation is 'to recognize that we have to live in the world *etsi deus non daretur*'.[25]

> God is teaching us that we must live as men who can get along very well without him. . . . This is the distinctive difference between Christianity and all religions. Man's religiosity makes him look back in his distress to the power of God in the world; he uses God as a *Deus ex machina*. The Bible however directs him to the powerlessness and suffering of God; only a suffering God can help. To this extent we may say that the process we have described by which the world came of age was an abandonment of a false conception of God, and a clearing of the decks for the God of the Bible, who conquers power and space in the world by his weakness. This must be the starting-point for our 'worldly interpretation'.[26]

[22] *Letters and Papers*, p. 108.
[23] *Idem, loc. cit.*   [24] *Ibid.*, p. 112.   [25] *Ibid.*, p. 121.
[26] *Ibid.*, p. 122; cf. also p. 125: 'This is what I mean by worldliness – taking

Dietrich Bonhoeffer's thesis has been developed very accurately by the American religious sociologist Peter L. Berger, especially in his book, *The Precarious Vision*.[27] The most recent exponent of the Bonhoeffer perspective is Paul Van Buren, whose book, *The Secular Meaning of the Gospel*,[28] attempts in a very original fashion to do justice to an orthodox Christology based on Barth as well as Bonhoeffer, and at the same time takes into account the philosophical critique of Wittgenstein and the linguistic analysts. We shall return to this work later in the chapter.

THE CHURCH AS MISSIONARY COMMUNITY ACCORDING TO BISHOP ROBINSON

If *Honest to God* is read in the light of the state-of-the-question outlined in the preceding section as well as in the context of Bishop Robinson's earlier writings, a great amount of misunderstanding and misinterpretation can be averted. First of all, Robinson readily admits that in this book he is 'struggling to think other people's thoughts after them'.[29] Those people are Bonhoeffer, Bultmann, and Tillich, especially – but certainly not exclusively. Secondly, he insists that he is writing *Honest to God* not as a professional theologian but rather as 'an ordinary churchman, and one moreover who is very much an "insider" as far as church membership is concerned.'[30] While this might very well be the case, most of his earlier books and articles of a more academic nature are presupposed throughout.

Bishop Robinson agrees that we are at the dawn of a new age, that 'we stand on the brink of a period in which it is going to become increasingly difficult to know what the true defence of Christian truth requires. . . . I believe we are being called, over the years ahead, to far more than a restating of traditional orthodoxy in

---

life in one's stride, with all its duties and problems, its successes and its failures, its experiences and helplessness. It is in such a life that we throw ourselves utterly into the arms of God and participate in his sufferings in the world and watch with Christ in Gethsemane.'

[27] Cf. pp. 123–125, 146–160, 164–167, 171.
[28] London, SCM Press, 1963.
[29] *Honest to God*, p. 21 (hereafter referred to as *HTG*).
[30] *HTG*, pp. 26–27.

modern terms. . . . A much more radical recasting, I would judge, is demanded, in the process of which the most fundamental categories of our theology – of God, of the supernatural, and of religion itself – must go into the melting.'[31]

This 'new age' is marked by a growing gulf between 'traditional orthodox supernaturalism' and the categories of thought which are meaningful to the 'lay' world of today. But *Honest to God*, as Robinson is quick to point out,[32] is not meant as a polemic against the traditionalists so much as a defence of the new apologetics. And in this delicate task the bishop admits to no fear of being too radical. On the contrary, 'the one thing of which I am fairly sure is that, in retrospect, it will be seen to have erred in not being nearly radical enough'.[33]

He willingly admits, however, that he approaches this project reluctantly ('It is for me a reluctant revolution'[34]), and as one who 'never really doubted the fundamental truth of the Christian faith – though I have constantly found myself questioning its expression'.[35] But a 'revolution' none the less it is. For just as the believer gradually withdrew from the concept of the God '*up* there' in a three-storied universe, so, too, must the believer today – in a world come of age – willingly relinquish the equally unacceptable concept of a God '*out* there', a Being separate from the world of reality, a distinct Person:

> The abandonment of a God 'out there' represents a much more radical break than the transition to this concept from that of a God 'up there'. For this earlier transposition was largely a matter of verbal

[31] *HTG*, p. 7.

[32] *Idem:* 'There are always those (and doubtless rightly they will be in the majority) who see the best, and indeed the only, defence of doctrine to lie in the firm reiteration, in fresh and intelligent contemporary language, of "the faith once delivered to the saints". And the Church has not lacked in recent years theologians and apologists who have given themselves to this task. Their work has been rewarded by a hungry following, and there will always be need of more of them. Nothing that I go on to say should be taken to deny their indispensable vocation.'

[33] *HTG*, p. 10; cf. also *The Honest to God Debate*, p. 250, where Bishop Robinson refers to Paul Van Buren's *The Secular Meaning of the Gospel* in these terms: 'I believe it is a major contribution and may already bear out my conviction that in retrospect *Honest to God* "will be seen to have erred in not being nearly radical enough".'

[34] *HTG*, p. 27.   [35] *Idem, loc. cit.*

notation, of a change in spatial metaphor, important as this undoubtedly
was in liberating Christianity from a flat-earth cosmology. But to be
asked to give up any idea of a Being 'out there' at all will appear to
be an outright denial of God. For, to the ordinary way of thinking, to
believe in God means to be convinced of the existence of such a supreme
and separate being. 'Theists' are those who believe that such a Being
exists, 'atheists' those who deny that he does.[36]

It was under the influence of Tillich that Bishop Robinson raised
his radical questions against the notion of the supranatural, the notion
of the God 'out there'; it was through Bonhoeffer that he was led to
question the notion of religion itself; and, finally, it was through the
stimulus of Bultmann's essay that he saw the relevance of the process
of demythologization to the whole problem of the re-structuring of
Christian theology. Robinson contends that these three theologians
speak to the modern world, despite the apparent difficulty of their
writings and their common Teutonic origin – and, one might add,
despite the fundamental differences that exist among them. Tillich
is one of 'the few theologians to have broken through . . . "the
theological circle". Bonhoeffer is talked of where "religion" does not
penetrate . . . [and] I was astonished to discover how Bultmann's
ideas, for all their forbidding jargon, seemed to come like a breath
of fresh air to entirely untheological students.'[37] This is not to
suggest, however, that the bishop has accepted all three uncritically,
as we shall see.

Robinson poses three basic questions that serve as his guide-lines
for formulating this new Christian apologetic, and he invokes Tillich
to answer the first, Bultmann for the second, and Bonhoeffer for the
third. The three questions are these: (1) Must Christianity be
'supranaturalist'? (2) Must Christianity be 'mythological'? (3) Must
Christianity be 'religious'?

(1) *Must Christianity be 'supranaturalist'?* According to Robinson, and
following Tillich, 'supranaturalism' is a way of thinking in which
'God is posited as "the highest Being" – out there, above and beyond
this world, existing in his own right alongside and over against his
creation.'[38] Furthermore, God is regarded as a separate Being whose

[36] *HTG*, p. 17.   [37] *HTG*, p. 25.
[38] *HTG*, p. 30. Robinson also defines 'supranaturalism' as a way of thinking
'by which the *reality* of God in human experience is represented by the *existence*

distinct existence must be demonstrated and established. For Tillich, and thus for Robinson, this is a false problem. 'Rather, we must start the other way round. God is, by definition, ultimate reality. And one cannot argue whether ultimate reality *exists*. One can only ask what ultimate reality is like. . . . Thus, the fundamental theological question consists not in establishing the "existence" of God as a separate entity but in pressing through in ultimate concern to what Tillich calls "the ground of our being".'[39] Such a transposition is necessary as an effective argument against the naturalism of a Julian Huxley who has insisted that the existence of a separate divine Being is superfluous because the world can be explained just as adequately without positing such a Being.

It is Tillich's particular contribution to our generation to have demonstrated 'that the Biblical faith in the reality of God can be stated in all its majesty and mystery, both of transcendence and immanence, without dependence on the supranaturalist scheme'.[40] 'Beyond this,' Robinson adds, 'I do not wish to be committed to Tillich's particular ontology.'[41]

(2) *Must Christianity be 'mythological'?* Bishop Robinson outlines the problem in this way:

> Behind such phrases as 'God created the heavens and the earth', or 'God came down from heaven', or 'God sent his only-begotten Son', lies a view of the world which portrays God as a person living in heaven, *a* God who is distinguished from the gods of the heathen by the fact that 'there is no god beside me'. . . .[42]
> Is it necessary for the Biblical faith to be expressed in terms of this world-view, which in its way is as primitive philosophically as the Genesis stories are primitive scientifically?[43]

---

of gods, or of a God in some other realm "above" or "beyond" the world in which we live'. Cf. *The New Reformation?*, p. 13, and *The Honest to God Debate*, p. 256.

[39] *HTG*, p. 29.   [40] *The Honest to God Debate*, p. 259.

[41] *Ibid.*, p. 260. Robinson's use of Tillich is especially evident in chapter 3 of *HTG*, 'The Ground of Our Being', pp. 45–63. As far back as 1950 Bishop Robinson was arguing for the use of philosophy and philosophical concepts in theology; cf. his review of Oscar Cullmann's *Christ and Time*, *Scottish Journal of Theology* 3 (1950) 86–89. Cf. also *The New Reformation?*, Appendix I, 'Can a Truly Contemporary Person *not* be an Atheist?', pp. 106–122.

[42] *HTG*, p. 32.   [43] *HTG*, p. 33.

Robinson endorses Bultmann's own response: 'There is nothing specifically Christian in the mythical view of the world as such. It is simply the cosmology of the pre-scientific age.'[44] Robinson proceeds to connect this insight with Tillich's when he interprets the Christ-event in these terms:

> In this person and event there was something of ultimate, uncondi-
> tional significance for human life – and that, translated into the
> mythological view of the world, comes out as 'God' (a Being up there)
> 'sending' (to 'this' world) his only-begotten 'Son'. The transcendental
> significance of the historical event is 'objectivized' as a supranatural
> transaction.[45]

Robinson's acceptance of the Bultmannian critique has by no means precluded a critique of his own vis-à-vis Bultmann's programme of demythologization. Bultmann, in Robinson's view, often reflects the scientific dogmatism of a previous generation, which gives to some of his exposition an air of old-fashioned modernism. Secondly, he is unwarrantably distrustful of the Gospel tradition, displaying excessive historical scepticism. Finally, his heavy reliance upon the particular philosophy of Heidegger's existentialism as a replacement for the mythological worldview is historically, as well as geographic-ally, conditioned. Robinson also agrees with Bonhoeffer's criticism of Bultmann, cited earlier in this chapter.[46]

(3) *Must Christianity be 'religious'?* With Bonhoeffer, Bishop Robinson identifies the God of 'religion' with a *Deus ex machina*, as the source of answers and explanations which are beyond our under-standing and our capacities to attain. 'But such a God', Robinson warns, 'is constantly pushed further and further back as the tide of secular studies advances. In science, in politics, in ethics, the need

---

[44] *HTG*, p. 34.   [45] *Idem, loc. cit.*

[46] For Robinson's own critique of Bultmann, cf. *HTG*, p. 35; cf. also his earlier review of Bultmann's *Theology of the New Testament*, 'The Hard Core of the Gospel: New Thought from Germany', *The Church of England Newspaper*, February 27, 1953: 'In the last resort Bultmann demythologizes because he does not like metaphysics. He believes, like Feuerbach, that theology must be reduced to anthropology: statements about God are really statements about "God as He is significant for man". But the question remains whether by the time he has finished there is any genuine history left. He makes Christ contemporary – but is He the Word made flesh, once?'

is no longer felt for such stop-gap or long-stop; he is not required in order to guarantee anything, to solve anything, or in any way to come to the rescue.'[47] In the words of Bonhoeffer himself: 'Man has learned to cope with all questions of importance without recourse to God as a working hypothesis.'[48] Robinson fully accepts Bonhoeffer's view that the 'religious premise' must be discarded even as St Paul had the courage to jettison circumcision as a precondition of the gospel and that the world's coming of age be accepted as a God-given fact.

To perpetuate the religious ideas against which Tillich, Bultmann and Bonhoeffer have argued is to perpetuate 'the greatest obstacle to an intelligent faith'. For 'if Christianity is to survive, let alone to recapture "secular" man, there is no time to lose in detaching it from this scheme of thought, from this particular theology or *logos* about *theos*, and thinking hard about what we should put in its place'.[49] 'Our concern', he insists, 'is in no way to change the Christian doctrine of God but precisely to see that it does not disappear with this outmoded view.'[50]

Of the various sources which Robinson employs in his book, the 'most radically original' contribution, in his judgement, is that offered by Dietrich Bonhoeffer.[51] For it was Bonhoeffer who insisted that Christ must be met at the centre of one's life. It was Bonhoeffer who took most seriously the secularity of modern man. For Robinson, therefore, *Honest to God* represents 'a dialogue between religious man and secular man. And secular man is just as much inside the Church as out of it, and just as much inside myself. Indeed my book was born of the fact that I knew myself to be a man committed without reservation to Christ *and* a man committed, without possibility of return, to modern twentieth-century secular society. It was written

---

[47] *HTG*, p. 37.   [48] *HTG*, p. 36.

[49] *HTG*, p. 43.

[50] *HTG*, p. 44. Robinson's use of Bonhoeffer is especially evident in chapters 4 and 5: 'The Man for Others' (pp. 64–83) and 'Worldly Holiness' (pp. 84–104). We have already discussed these areas of Bonhoeffer's thought in connection with our study of the Church as the secular community in the previous chapter. Cf. also 'Communicating with the Contemporary Man,' *Religion in Television*, London: Independent Television Authority, 1964, pp. 27–35.

[51] *The Honest to God Debate*, pp. 271–272.

out of the belief that both these convictions must be taken with equal seriousness and that they *cannot* be incompatible.'[52]

The principal concern of *Honest to God*, as it should be evident, is with the *content* of the Church's missionary preaching. His understanding of the Church *as* a missionary community, however, is something that must be deduced from the book's various implicit assumptions. The Church must indeed preach the gospel and, as a bishop, he must be its 'guardian and defender'.[53] But the Church need not be – and, in fact, often *must* not be – tied exclusively to the traditional imagery and symbolism of the Bible or credal formulations. Finally, it is also implied that, since not all men are called to membership in the Church (what he would later refer to as the 'manifest' Church), the Church's missionary preaching need not terminate in successes of a quantitative nature.

But what is merely implied in *Honest to God* is stated somewhat more openly in its sequel, *The New Reformation?* The Church exists as the Son of Man on earth. It is a *secular* community even as it is a *missionary* community. In its preaching of the gospel, it must give witness to the Christ, the 'gracious neighbour', the 'man for others'. 'Perhaps the primary task of theology and of the Church in our generation', the bishop states, 'could be described as making such a meeting possible again.'[54] The characteristic of this missionary community is 'that it is prepared to meet men *where they are* and accept them *for what they are*'.[55] For the question 'insistently posed by the Gospels is not how far men are from the manifest Church but how far they are from the kingdom of God.'[56] The manifest Church does not exist primarily as 'the organized centre *into* which to draw men', for 'its *normal* form of existence, when it is distinctively being itself, is *not* to be gathered together in one place, but to be embedded as seeds of light within the dark world. And, within this world, by no means its only job is to make more Christians, that is, more members of the manifest Church. Yet this is regularly assumed to be the goal

---

[52] *The Honest to God Debate*, p. 275. A discussion of Bishop Robinson's moral theology is outside the scope of this study: cf. *Christian Morals Today*, London: SCM Press, 1964, and *HTG*, chapter 6, 'The New Morality' (pp. 105–121).

[53] *HTG*, p. 7.   [54] *The New Reformation?*, p. 37.
[55] *Ibid.*, p. 46.   [56] *Ibid.*, p. 48.

to which the whole of the Church's mission is geared.'[57] On the contrary, the Church must simply allow Christ to be met as Son of Man *incognito*, that is, 'in an utterly disinterested concern for persons for their own sake, and in relationships that have nothing distinctively religious about them'.[58] Robinson strenuously denies that this is 'reducing' the gospel to mere humanism and 'giving in' to secularism, as many of his critics have charged. On the contrary, these are the only forms under which it is possible to communicate the things of God to the majority of men and women in our contemporary secularized world. We must preach a 'Jesus come, and coming, in the flesh'.[59] We must permit a man to be a Christian without forcing him to feel that in order to do so he must go back upon the age to which he belongs and embrace the equivalent of a 'medieval' worldview. 'I am profoundly convinced', he writes, 'that a truly contemporary person *can* be a Christian, but not if his acceptance of the Faith is *necessarily* tied to certain traditional thought-forms – metaphysical, supranaturalistic, mythological and religious – against which secularization marks a decisive revolt.'[60] This does not entail a watering down of the gospel but its renewal, so that it might be able to come to men *as good news*.[61]

A CRITICAL EVALUATION

It must be pointed out at the very beginning that the various critical reactions to *Honest to God* have concentrated their attention on Robinson's presentation of the *content* of the missionary preaching rather than the underlying ecclesiological assumptions. This is entirely understandable in view of the nature of the book itself. Accordingly, our consideration of these reviews will be brief, if not superficial.

Much of the earliest reaction was of a negative character, as might have been expected. Robinson was accused of atheism,[62] of 'an

---

[57] *The New Reformation?*, p. 48.   [58] *Ibid.*, p. 50.   [59] *Ibid.*, p. 51.
[60] *Ibid.*, p. 52.

[61] The reader is referred back to the previous chapter where this material is presented more fully, although in a slightly different context.

[62] Cf., for example, *The Honest to God Debate*, p. 215.

arbitrary and untraditional use of the expression (religionless Christianity), fraught with possibilities of misunderstanding',[63] of heresy and 'non-sense',[64] and of a lack of a sense of history.[65] None of these opinions, with the possible exception of the last, seems at all justifiable, as Bishop Robinson himself takes pains to make clear in his most recent book:

> I have not the least desire to weaken or deny the distinctive affirmations of the Christian faith. Among these I should certainly wish to assert: (1) The centrality of the confession 'Jesus is Lord', in the full New Testament sense that 'in him all things cohere' (Col. 1.17) and 'in him the whole fulness of the deity dwells bodily' (Col. 2.9); and (2) the centrality of the utterly *personal* relationship of communion with God summed up in Jesus' address 'Abba, Father!'[66]

Other reviews, among Catholics especially, have ranged from sympathetic criticism to outright endorsement.[67] There are two reviews of particular value, however; namely, that of A. Van den Heuvel, 'The Honest to God Debate in Ecumenical Perspective',[68] and that of E. Schillebeeckx in the Dutch theological journal, *Tijdschrift voor Theologie*.[69]

Van de Heuvel's fundamental criticism is well made: 'The inconsistency of the book and the many self-contradictions in it are not a result of heresy, but the consequence of a desire to systematize.

[63] C. Ryan, 'Religionless Christianity', *Blackfriars* 45 (1964) 242–257, cf. p. 256.

[64] O. Fielding Clarke, *For Christ's Sake*, Wallington: Religious Education Press, 1963, pp. 11 and 41, *et passim*.

[65] A. Richardson, 'God: Our Search or His?' in *Four Anchors from the Stern*, London: SCM Press, 1963, pp. 5–14; cf. also C. C. West, 'The Obsolescence of History', *The Ecumenical Review* 17 (1965) 1–17, especially pp. 7–8.

[66] *The New Reformation?*, p. 13. Nevertheless, he continues to insist that we must be agnostic about many doctrines 'at the borders' (pp. 23–24) and that we must work toward a new formulation of Christian doctrine (pp. 80 ff.).

[67] Cf. T. Merton, 'The Honest-to-God Debate,' *Commonweal* 80 (1964) 573–578; G. Baum, ' "Honest to God" and Traditional Theology', *Ecumenist* 2 (1964) 65–68; and P. Cren, 'Etre Honnête envers Dieu,' *Lumière et Vie* 13 (1964) 93–104.

[68] *Ecumenical Review* 16 (1964) 279–294.

[69] 'Evangelische zuiverheid en menselijke waarachtigheid,' *Tijdschrift voor Theologie* 3 (1963) 283–326, and 'Het interpretatie van het geloof in het licht van de seculariteit,' *ibid.*, 4 (1964) 109–150. A significantly sympathetic review was produced recently by F. C. Copleston, S. J., 'Probe at Woolwich', *The Month*, June, 1965. Of some significance, too, is the *neutral* review by C. Boyer, S.J., in *Osservatore Romano*, June 18, 1965, p. 2.

That seems to me the real weakness of *Honest to God*: it does not pay sufficient attention to the fragmentary nature of our actual under-standing.'[70] This would certainly explain Robinson's rather super-ficial handling of Tillich and Bultmann especially, and then grouping them in an implausible alliance with Bonhoeffer. Van den Heuvel also suggests Christology as the logical starting-point, as a corrective to the bishop's apparent reduction of theology to anthropology. Robinson seems to take this view into account in *The New Reformation?* where his Son-of-Man Christology is paramount. We must reserve final judgement on Robinson's Christology because it is hardly sufficiently developed. At first glance, however, it appears to suffer from the same weakness which affects Bonhoeffer's doctrine of Christ. As Jaroslav Pelikan has accurately observed, Bonhoeffer barely extricates himself from the Ebionite heresy with his pre-occupation with the concreteness of Jesus Christ.[71]

Schillebeeckx, on the other hand, approaches the issues raised by Bishop Robinson with the categories of the vertical and horizontal dimensions of the Christian life. It is true, he notes, that our experi-ence of God is only indirect, that the acknowledgement of his existence is correlative with the affirmation of our contingent existence in the world. God is the transcendent third in all our dealings with earthly reality, especially with other men. But even in being the Ground and Creator of man and the world, God is recognized as being transcendent. This is the vertical dimension. But there is also a horizontal notion of transcendence which consists in a real but powerless longing to encounter God himself in a truly personal relationship. Thus, man's cultural activities in this world leave him basically unsatisfied *as a person*. Man's religious intention or tendency cannot take place in this life on a purely horizontal level.

How might the relationship between God and man be more properly described? God wishes to enter into an intimate I–Thou relationship with man, but he cannot do this without respecting the

[70] *Ecumenical Review* 16, p. 292.

[71] 'Bonhoeffer's *Christologie*', in *The Place of Bonhoeffer*, p. 164. The Ebionites were a Jewish-Christian sect which observed the Mosaic Law and regarded Paul as an apostate from the faith. They denied the divinity of Christ, insisting instead that he was a man elected by God for a particular mission.

condition of man, that is to say, God must enter man's own framework, namely the context of saving history. It is only in the personal
encounter with the man Jesus in his Church that the authentic
experience of God's intimacy is properly and fully given.   This
intimacy with God demands both a sacral and a secular soil in which
to grow and develop. The sacral soil is provided by the Church and
its Sacred Scriptures, preaching, the sacraments, and so forth. The
secular soil consists in the Christian responsibility to the world. These
two levels cannot be separated, though it is entirely possible to place
the emphasis on one or the other. *Honest to God* stresses an aspect that
was too long forgotten in theology and in Christian life, namely the
horizontal dimension. 'But, on the other hand,' he concludes, 'he
has not done justice to the *proper value* of being-together and working-
together with the living God. He has put the entire stress on the
secular implications of religion, but in this way he has lost sight of
its eschatological meaning, and so cut out its heart, if one may judge
from his explicit assertions. What he really wants is making the
Church of Christ into a genuine community of fully human love.'[72]

In the final analysis, however, the real substance of our position
on Bishop Robinson's concept of the Church as the missionary
community is contained in the judgements we expressed in the
previous chapter. It is beyond the scope of this investigation to
examine the *content* of the missionary preaching which the bishop
proposes, except in so far as this content refers specifically, or at least
indirectly, to his doctrine of the Church. Taking into account the
reservations we have formulated throughout this study, we are
inclined, none the less, to pass a favourable judgement on the
ecclesiological assumptions which underlie his idea of the missionary
community. The Church must, indeed, preach the gospel to all
mankind, but it must preach this message in the light of the real
situation, in the light of the phenomenon of secularization. The
Church cannot give proper witness (*marturia*) to Christ apart from

---

[72] *Tijdschrift voor Theologie* 3, p. 326; cf. also his *Christ the Sacrament of Encounter
with God*, especially the first two chapters, pp. 5–109. Schillebeeckx's criticism, of
course, cannot stand when measured against Bishop Robinson's other writings,
where he neither puts the entire stress on the secular implications of religion nor
loses sight of its eschatological meaning.

her mission of service (*diakonia*) in the world and for the sake of the Kingdom. And neither of these functions will matter at all unless the whole thrust and impulse of her life work to the building up of the community as such (*koinonia*). As Yves Congar has written:

> The World Council of Churches has made these three terms the foundation, as it were the tripod on which its programme of action stands, and by so doing has gone straight to the heart of truth in its most authentic form.
>
> These three supreme realities could be the starting-point of a positive programme of Christian life in the world. The demands they make would not only affect individuals, but the Church herself, *qua* Church, and hence at the ecclesiological level.[73]

One need only examine once again the design on his episcopal pectoral cross to be assured that these realities are central to Bishop Robinson's own ecclesiological thought.[74]

[73] *Power and Poverty in the Church*, pp. 137–138.

[74] See pp. 11–12 above, and cf. *Liturgy Coming to Life*, p. xii, as well as his letter of September 24, 1964: 'The design on the front of the English cover of the second edition of *Liturgy Coming to Life* . . . reproduces the design on my pectoral cross, with an explanation inside. The two sides of this sum up pictorially a good many of the things that seem to me central.'

7

CONCLUSION

IT would be superfluous and unduly repetitious to summarize
the entire discussion at this point. Adequate résumés occur at
various significant junctures of this study. The point of these
final pages is simply to bring together in synthetic form the various
critical conclusions that have been reached, if only tentatively,
throughout this investigation.

First of all, it should be recalled that this project was undertaken
with full knowledge of the risks involved. John A. T. Robinson is not
a professional dogmatic theologian, nor has he ever attempted to
produce a systematic ecclesiology. Yet it should now be evident, in
retrospect, that, apart from certain specifically exegetical studies,
he has always been engaged in the theological enterprise. And while
he has not given us a systematic exposition of his doctrine of the
Church, his writings of an ecclesiological interest – and these are
clearly in the majority – are sufficiently consistent and explicit to
allow one to develop a synthesis by induction.

Yet the fact remains – and this is our second point – that Bishop
Robinson is not a systematic theologian with impressive academic
credentials. Accordingly, much of his work – and especially that
beyond the range of his exegetical competence – labours under the
burden of a certain superficiality which is usually manifested in at
least two ways: (1) in the obvious lack of acquaintance with certain
important areas of theological research (the neglect of significant
Catholic sources is a case in point, but by no means the only one);
and (2) in the 'patch-work' fashion in which he sometimes assembles

and employs his sources (for example, his use of Bonhoeffer, Bult-mann, and Tillich in *Honest to God*). Both these deficiencies are especially apparent in his two most recent books, but they are also in evidence in *The Body* – a book hastily written and with noticeable bibliographical gaps.

Thirdly, there is some question, too, about the actual theology that develops in the course of his writings. If the episcopacy is only of the *plene esse* of the Church, what *is* the structural place of the apostolic college? Is there really no essential distinction between the priest-hood of the ordained and the priesthood of all the faithful?

Fourthly, there are unsettling doubts that tend to arise about the central area of Christology in Bishop Robinson's thought. Does he not insist too strongly that Christ made no claims about himself? Would not an 'adoptionist' Christology, if pushed to extremes, upset the delicate ecclesiological balance already achieved? It is difficult to do more than pose the question, because the bishop simply has not developed a Christology that is sufficiently viable to criticize.

Fifthly, John A. T. Robinson is first and foremost a man *of* his times and a Christian sensitive *to* his times. As a man *of* his times he has come under the strong influence of the 'obvious' people, of Bonhoeffer, Tillich, Cullmann, Dodd, and others. But in an effort to systematize them at certain delicate points, he has produced certain discrepancies and ambiguities in his own thought. On the other hand, he is a man isolated – at least up until very recent times – from the broad and increasingly vibrant current of Catholic theological thought that has been developing since the Second World War.

He is also a Christian sensitive *to* his times and remarkably conscious of the fact that the world has indeed 'come of age'. Thus, pastoral concerns have always remained uppermost in his mind and even in his most serious theological work. His consecration as Bishop of Woolwich has accentuated this direction of thought and has, in fact, rendered it irreversible. That is why Bishop Robinson will never, in all probability, produce a systematic exposition of his doctrine of the Church, or any other significant area of his theology for that matter. Yet at this stage in the history of theology such systematization, at least in the present area of his concern – the mission of the Church – is hardly possible. It is a developing, but still underdeveloped, area of ecclesiology.

When all is said and done, John A. T. Robinson is an important figure indeed in contemporary Christian theology. However one might ultimately judge his extraordinarily best-selling *Honest to God*, neither the book nor its author can simply be dismissed. Robinson has become important not only for what he has himself produced, but even more because of what he represents. His writings suggest a theology in crisis, just as his pastoral work suggests a Church in crisis, on the verge, perhaps, of a new reformation. To have ignored him would be to have ignored one of the most significant phenomena of our day.

In this time of change and crisis it is absolutely imperative that the question of the nature and mission of the Church be clearly and boldly confronted. Bishop Robinson is to be commended for his unequivocal insistence that ecclesiology is impossible without an eschatology, that the Church must always subject herself to the demands of the Kingdom. And he is to be commended in a particular manner for dramatizing and developing the rich insights of Dietrich Bonhoeffer with regard to the notion of the Servant Church in a newly secularized world. In a sense, Robinson is a 'high-church' version of Bonhoeffer. Without this theological ingredient, Bonhoeffer remains woefully inadequate ecclesiologically. Robinson, therefore, has a definite contribution to make to this new ferment that has been developing of late in mid-twentieth century Christianity. As a 'radical' he is decidedly a man of *roots* and his doctrine of the Church, however inadequate it might be from the Catholic standpoint, is a stable and integral part of those roots. Indeed, the disastrous consequences of an uncertain ecclesiological perspective are manifested very strikingly in the aforementioned book by Paul Van Buren, *The Secular Meaning of the Gospel*. For Van Buren the Church is simply 'the company of those sharing (a common) perspective'. The 'Body of Christ' is 'obviously not a description (but) a reference to the historical perspective which the members presumably have in common, and it suggests the harmony that would exist between people who shared this perspective'.[1] And as for the Church's *mission*,

[1] P. 183.

it is to 'claim the world for Christ', which means 'simply that the whole world may be seen with the Christian's perspective'. The Christian 'need not ask nor expect the world to understand itself as he understands it. Since he has acquired this perspective in connection with a freedom which is contagious, he should be content to let this contagion work its own way in the world, without his taking thought for the morrow, especially the morrow of the church.'[2] Van Buren, and all others with similar laudable concerns, would profit from a reading of John A. T. Robinson – a reading that extends far beyond the limited confines of *Honest to God!*

In his inaugural lecture at Cambridge University, C. H. Dodd offered his own definition of the 'ideal interpreter' of the New Testament. Robinson, in a recent article on Dodd, suggests that the description would apply pre-eminently to Dodd himself. I am inclined to think that it would apply equally well to the Bishop of Woolwich, for it explains much of the life, writings, and concerns of John A. T. Robinson:

> The ideal interpreter would be one who has entered into that strange first-century world, has felt its whole strangeness, has sojourned in it until he has lived himself into it, thinking and feeling as one of those to whom the Gospel first came, and who will then return into our world, and give to the truth he has discerned a body out of the stuff of our own thought.[3]

[2] Pp. 190–192. Cf. Bishop Robinson's own critique of Van Buren in *The Honest to God Debate*, pp. 249 ff.

[3] Cited by Robinson in 'Theologians of Our Time: C. H. Dodd,' *The Expository Times* 75 (1964) 102.

BIBLIOGRAPHY

Books, articles and pamphlets by Bishop John A. T. Robinson
to the end of 1965

1945

'The Religious Foundation of the University', *The Cambridge Review*, January 20, 1945
'Agape and Eros', *Theology* 48 (1945) 98–104
Thou Who Art: The notion of personality and its relation to Christian theology with particular reference to (a) the contemporary 'I–Thou' philosophy; (b) the doctrines of the Trinity and the Person of Christ, Cambridge University, 1945 (unpublished)

1947

'The Temptations', *Theology* 50 (1947) 43–48 (reprinted: *Twelve New Testament Studies*, pp. 53–60)

1948

'Hosea and the Virgin Birth', *Theology* 52 (1948) 373–375

1949

'Universalism – Is it Heretical?', *Scottish Journal of Theology* 2 (1949) 139–155

1950

Review of Oscar Cullmann's *Christ and Time*, *Scottish Journal of Theology* 3 (1950) 86–89
'The House Church and the Parish Church', *Theology* 53 (1950) 283–287 (reprinted: *On Being the Church in the World*, pp. 83–95)
In the End, God . . .: A Study of the Christian Doctrine of the Last Things, London: James Clarke, 1950 (new edition to appear in the series *Perspectives in Humanism*, New York: Harper & Row, 1967)

1952

The Body: A Study in Pauline Theology (Studies in Biblical Theology, no. 5), London: SCM Press, 1952
'The Theological College in a Changing World', *Theology* 55 (1952) 202–207
'The Social Content of Salvation', *Frontier*, November, 1952 (reprinted: *On Being the Church in the World*, pp. 23–30)

1953

Review of Rudolf Bultmann's *Theology of the New Testament*, vol. I, *The Church of England Newspaper*, February 27, 1953

Review of J. Marsh's *The Fulness of Time*, *Theology* 56 (1953) 107–109

'Traces of a Liturgical Sequence in 1 Cor. 16, 20–24', *Journal of Theological Studies* n.s. 4 (1953) 38–41 (reprinted: *Twelve New Testament Studies*, pp. 154–157, with the new title, 'The Earliest Christian Liturgical Sequence?')

'The Gospel and Race', *The Church of England Newspaper*, July 24, 1953 (reprinted: *On Being the Church in the World*, pp. 116–120)

Review of Oscar Cullmann's *Peter: Disciple, Apostle, Martyr*, *The Church of England Newspaper*, September 7, 1953

'The One Baptism as a Category of New Testament Soteriology', *Scottish Journal of Theology* 6 (1953) 257–274 (reprinted: *Twelve New Testament Studies*, pp. 158–175)

'The Christian Hope' in *Christian Faith and Communist Faith* (ed. D. M. Mackinnon), London: Macmillan, 1953, pp. 209–226

1954

'Our Present Position in the Light of the Bible', in *Becoming a Christian* (ed. B. Minchin), London: Faith Press, 1954, pp. 48–57

'Kingdom, Church and Ministry', in *The Historic Episcopate in the Fulness of the Church* (ed. K. M. Carey), London: Dacre Press, 1954 (2nd ed., 1960), pp. 11–12

'Trusting the Universe':
(1) 'The Faith of the Scientist'
(2) 'The Faith of the Philosopher'
(3) 'The Faith of the Christian', *The Church of England Newspaper*, September 17 and 24, October 1, 1954

Review of J. Knox's *Chapters in a Life of Paul*, *The Church of England Newspaper*, October 29, 1954

Review of J. Jeremias' *The Parables of Jesus*, *The Church of England Newspaper*, November 26, 1954

1955

'The Parable of the Shepherd (John 10, 1–5)', *Zeitschrift für die neutestamentliche Wissenschaft* 46 (1955) 233–240 (reprinted: *Twelve New Testament Studies*, pp. 67–75)

Review of E. Best's *One Body in Christ*, *Theology* 58 (1955) 391–393

Review of V. Taylor's *The Life and Ministry of Jesus*, *New Testament Studies* 2 (1955) 148–149

1956

'The "Parable" of the Sheep and the Goats', *New Testament Studies* 2 (1956) 225–237 (reprinted: *Twelve New Testament Studies*, pp. 76–93)

'The Second Coming – Mk. xiv, 62', *The Expository Times* 67 (1956) 336–340

'The Most Primitive Christology of All?', *Journal of Theological Studies* 7 (1956) 177–189 (reprinted: *Twelve New Testament Studies*, pp. 139–153)

'The Historicity of the Gospels', in *Jesus Christ: History, Interpretation and Faith* (R. C. Walton, T. W. Manson, and John A. T. Robinson), London, SPCK, 1956, pp. 45–63

1957

'Intercommunion and Concelebration', *The Ecumenical Review* 9 (1957) 203–206 (reprinted: *On Being the Church in the World*, pp. 96–100)

'The Baptism of John and the Qumran Community', *Harvard Theological Review* 50 (1957) 175–191 (reprinted: *Twelve New Testament Studies*, pp. 11–27)

'Preaching Judgement', *The Preacher's Quarterly*, September and December, 1957 (reprinted: *On Being the Church in the World*, pp. 135–147)

Jesus and His Coming: The Emergence of a Doctrine, London: SCM Press, 1957

1958

'Elijah, John and Jesus: an essay in Detection,' *New Testament Studies* 4 (1958) 263–281 (reprinted: *Twelve New Testament Studies*, pp. 28–52)

'The Teaching of Theology for the Ministry', *Theology* 61 (1958) 486–495

1959

Review of W. D. Stacey's *The Pauline View of Man*, *Journal of Theological Studies* 10 (1959) 144–146

'The New Look on the Fourth Gospel', in *Studia Evangelica* (ed. K. Aland, et al.), Berlin: Akademie-Verlag, 1959, pp. 510–515 (reprinted: *The Gospels Reconsidered. A Selection of Papers read at the International Congress on The Four Gospels in* 1957, Oxford: Blackwell, 1960, pp. 154–166, and *Twelve New Testament Studies*, pp. 94–106)

'The "Others" of John 4, 38', in *Studia Evangelica* (ed. K. Aland, et al.), Berlin: Akademie-Verlag, 1959, pp. 510–515 (reprinted: *Twelve New Testament Studies*, pp. 61–66)

'Episcopacy and Intercommunion', *Theology* 62 (1959) 402–408 (reprinted: *On Being the Church in the World*, pp. 101–109)

1960

'The Destination and Purpose of St John's Gospel', *New Testament Studies* 6 (1960) 117–131 (reprinted: *Twelve New Testament Studies*, pp. 107–125)

Review of *The Biblical Doctrine of Baptism* (Commission on Baptism, Church of Scotland, Edinburgh, 1959) in *Scottish Journal of Theology* 13 (1960) 99–102

On Being the Church in the World, London: SCM Press, 1960

Christ Comes In, London: Mowbray, 1960

'The Destination and Purpose of the Johannine Epistles', *New Testament Studies* 7 (1960–1) 56–65 (reprinted: *Twelve New Testament Studies*, pp. 126–138)

Liturgy Coming to Life, London: Mowbray, 1960 (2nd edition with new preface, 1963)

'Taking the Lid off the Church's Ministry', in *New Ways with the Ministry*, London: Faith Press, 1960, pp. 9–21

1961

'A New Model of Episcopacy', in *Bishops: what they are and what they do* (ed. the Bishop of Llandaff), London: Faith Press, 1961, pp. 125–138

1962

Twelve New Testament Studies (Studies in Biblical Theology, no. 34), London: SCM Press, 1962

'The Church of England and Intercommunion', *Prism* 4 (1962), no. 3, pp. 3–15 (reprinted: as Prism Pamphlet no. 2, London, 1962)

'Resurrection in the NT', in *The Interpreter's Dictionary of the Bible* (vol. IV), New York and Nashville: Abingdon Press, 1962, pp. 43–53

'Five Points for Christian Action', in *Man and Society* 2 (1962) 13–15

'The Significance of the Foot-Washing', in *Neotestamentica et Patristica: Eine Freundesgabe, Herrn Professor Dr Oscar Cullmann zu seinem 60. Geburtstag überreicht*, Leiden: E. J. Brill, 1962, pp. 144–147

1963

'The Relation of the Prologue to the Gospel of St John', *New Testament Studies* 9 (1962–3) 120–129 (reprinted: *The Authorship and Integrity of the New Testament*, London: SPCK, 1965, pp. 61–72)

'The Tercentenary of the Book of Common Prayer', in *Parish and People*, no. 36 (Epiphany, 1963), pp. 15–19

'On Being a Radical', *The Listener*, February 21, 1963

'Our Image of God must Go', *The Observer*, March 17, 1963 (reprinted in *The Observer Revisited*, London: Hodder & Stoughton, 1964, pp. 42–47)

Honest to God, London: SCM Press, 1963

The World That God Loves (pamphlet), London: Church Missionary Society, 1963 (reprinted: *The Episcopal Overseas Mission Review* 10 [1965], no. 3, 2–7)

Keeping in Touch with Theology (pamphlet), London: SCM Press, 1963 (reprinted from *Twentieth Century*, summer, 1963)

'The Ministry and the Laity', in *Layman's Church* (ed. T. W. Beaumont), London: Lutterworth Press, 1963, pp. 9–22

The Honest to God Debate (ed. John A. T. Robinson and D. L. Edwards), London: SCM Press, 1963, pp. 228–279

'Der Verpflichtung der Kirche gegenüber dem Menschen der Gegenwart', *Monatschrift für Pastoral Theologie* 52 (1963) 321–328

'The Place of the Fourth Gospel', in *The Roads Converge: A Contribution to the Question of Christian Reunion* (ed. P. Gardner-Smith), London: Arnold, 1963, pp. 49–74

'The Great Benefice Barrier', *Prism*, no. 80 (December, 1963) 4–13

1964

'Our Common Reformation', *Catholic Gazette* 55, no. 1 (January 1964) 6–7

'Theologians of Our Time: C. H. Dodd', *The Expository Times* 75 (1964) 100–102 (reprinted: *Theologians of Our Time* ed. A. W. and E. Hastings, Edinburgh: T. & T. Clark, 1966, pp. 40–46; and in *Tendenzen der Theologie im 20. Jahrhundert* [ed. H. J. Schultz], Stuttgart: Kreuz-Verlag, 1966)

Christian Morals Today, London: SCM Press, 1964

'Communicating with the Contemporary Man', in *Religion in Television*, London: Independent Television Authority, 1964, pp. 27–35

''Η ἠθική κρίση καί ἡ ἠθική ἀξίωση, Εποχες (Athens) 18 (October, 1964) 3–6

'Ascendancy', *Andover Newton Quarterly* n.s. 5 (1964) 5–9 (reprinted: *The Pulpit* 36 (1965), no. 5, 4–6; and, with the title 'The Ascendancy of Christ', *Pulpit Digest* 45 (1965), no. 321, 45–48)

'Curiouser and Curiouser: Reflections of a Bemused Suffragan', *Prism*, no. 92 (December, 1964) 33–34

1965

'Rocking the Radical Boat Too', *Prism*, no. 95 (March 1965), 6–10

'Can a Truly Contemporary Person *not* be an Atheist?', *The Sunday Times*, March 14, 1965 (reprinted in *The New Reformation?*, pp. 106–122)

The New Reformation?, London: SCM Press, 1965

'Can Anglicanism Survive? Death and Resurrection', *New Statesman*, April 9, 1965

'Living with Sex', *The Observer*, June 13, 1965

'. . . And What Next . . .'?, *Prism*, no. 101 (September, 1965) 9–17

'God Dwelling Incognito', *New Christian*, October 7, 1965

'Bearing the Reality of Christmas', *New Christian*, December 16, 1965

INDEX OF PROPER NAMES

INDEX OF SUBJECTS